Meeting

In

The

Middle

Stories that Bless Souls

Book Compilation Visionary and Publisher

Tanicia "Shamay Speaks" Currie

Mother~Author~Publisher~Event Planner/Host~Entrepreneur

925-421-0221

Shamayspeaks@gmail.com

www.WriteItAwayPublishing.com

978-0-9966729-4-8

COPYRIGHT 2017 by Tanicia Shamay Currie/ Write It Away Publishing

All rights reserved. No part of this book may be reproduced or transmitted in any form or by any means, electronic or mechanical, except for permitted in Section 107 or 108 of the 1976 United States Copyright Act, without prior written consent of the publisher except for the inclusion of brief quotes in a review. While the author and the publisher have used their best efforts in preparing this book, they make no representations or warranties with respect to the accuracy or completeness of the contents of this book.

Synopsis:

Meeting in the Middle is an inspirational short story book that features women and men who decided it was time to tell their story. Each person in this world is a soul and each story is meant to bless a soul. Often times in society we may feel that women may have more stories, but make no mistake: God doesn't discriminate when He lays out our divine path, whether you're a man or woman. In this book, women and men stepped out on faith, decided to meet in the middle, and join forces to share their story with the world to bless another soul. Chapter by chapter, this collection of stories will speak to many of us and touch our souls.

Table of Contents

Foreword 1

About the Book's Visionary 5

Introduction 7

Discovering & Pursuing My Purpose 11

Chapter 1: Elementary to High School
By Holly Cranshaw... 12

Broken To Resilient 27

Chapter 2: I Rise
By Briggette Rockett, M.Ed 28

If My Story Inspires One Person Then My Job is Done! 47

Chapter 3: God Moments
By Vanessa Oden 48

My Mess Turned Into My MESSage 65

Chapter 4: Walk of Worship
By Benjamin L. Rivera 66

Chapter 5: "The Beginning of a Destiny Begins With Tearing Down"
By Dannielle Hart 80

Chapter 6: "Balance"
By Anonymous.. 94

Chapter 7: "The Lives He Lived"
By Tanicia "Shamay Speaks" Currie 105

The Take Away (Epilogue) 119

Foreword

I was elated when I learned I had been chosen by Tanicia to write the foreword for her for next book, *Meeting in the Middle*. Tanicia could have chosen so many others, but I am truly grateful for the opportunity. I was introduced to Tanicia by my little sister in the Christian faith, Monique. Monique was preparing to attend Tanicia's self-publishing workshop.

Monique called and said, "Sis there are two more spots available in the 2016 self-publishing workshop, and you should consider being a part of it". Monique thought it might be time for me to gain the wisdom I needed to help me prepare for some of my own projects. Monique would always share her enthusiasm from attending Tanicia's workshops, so I began to get interested and excited.

My excitement would soon deflate, as I remembered what the inside of my wallet looked like. Within less than a year, the same opportunity presented itself again, and this time I had the resources and everything fell into place.

Tanicia is first and foremost a very professional business woman. Tanicia's self-publishing workshops are comprehensive, and the tools she gives her clients in her author's workshops set them up for success. I have worked with women professionally for over thirty years. What I respect about Tanicia is the safe, non-judgmental environment she creates for her writers.

During the workshop, Tanicia had some of her published books on display so the authors could understand the process. She gave us opportunities to read her work during some of the breaks in between segments. The book I was drawn to by the cover alone was "Red Flags: *Deep Within I Knew He Wasn't for Me*". I said to myself, "Hello! I could have written this a few times myself"! I fell in love with Tanicia's courage in her writing as she encourages her readers to benefit from self-examination in their personal lives, which I believe is very humbling. Self-examination can defuse that opportunity of having a false estimation of oneself, by passing the blame, and not owning up to one's part in a broken relationship.

I had no problem driving from San Jose, CA to Pittsburg, CA, a one hour and fifteen-minute drive to Tanicia's workshop. It was worth it to me, even when I was sure there were some author workshops in San Jose where I live. I'm glad I did not look anywhere else!

Not only did I received the knowledge I needed regarding self-publishing, writing styles and techniques, but I met some very amazing, talented, and gifted women as well. God is omniscient, He knows everything. He knows who to choose to bring the best out of you, and to release the wisdom to you for

Foreword

what you're doing. Tanicia was that for me, and I truly consider her one of my blessings in 2017. I didn't know the process or even where to start, or who to trust with the secrets I knew I would somehow have to share. So, I say "Thank you Lord for my little forerunner Monique", that would soon introduce me to Tanicia.

I was reading Zora Neale Hurston's book, Dust Tracks on The Road, and there's a quote in there that says, "Truth is like a letter of courage." I'm grateful for the wisdom and the knowledge that Tanicia's classes provide that allow me to write my letters of courage.

I have been blessed to have had this opportunity with such a creative, gifted, and talented author.

Chere' Sifflet

www.Penitmyway.com

About the Book's Visionary
Tanicia "Shamay Speaks" Currie

Tanicia "Shamay Speaks" Currie is a 35 year old single mother who does not believe in settling in life. Having faced many life challenges, including gearing up to have her 4th heart surgery in September of 2017, Tanicia feels that God definitely gave her a purpose. Growing up in a challenging environment with a drug addiction in her home, she convinced herself that there had to be more to life than those circumstances. Rather than allow her upbringing to dictate her success, she decided to turn her life's hardships into motivation to persevere in life. She became the first in her immediate family to graduate college with a bachelor's degree. In 2009, she went on to open Cause' N A Stir Entertainment, hosting events from concerts to fashion shows to annual toy drives. Tanicia is also the artist relations manager and organizer for the 9quota Awards, which is an annual award show that honors local arts and talents within her community. Her life changed in 2013 when her daughter Laniyah was born. Laniyah is the best blessing she ever received, but becoming a mother also showed her that it was time to kick life into overdrive. Tanicia is currently the CEO of Branches of Community Services, which helps her give back to those in need. In 2014, she decided to finish the book she started over 8 years prior. She published her first book titled "Deep Within I

Knew He Wasn't for Me" in October 2015. Tanicia is a featured author in two empowerment books, "Igniting The Vision" and "Stand Up Be Heard." Tanicia is currently working with women and men with her next book compilation, set to release January 2018. She enjoys assisting others with sharing their story and fulfilling their dream of becoming published authors. Her solo book will be released in 2018. Being passionate about empowering others to rise above their circumstances and take charge of their destiny, Tanicia's mission in life is to chase all that life has to offer, never give up, and stay humble. Tanicia truly hopes to use her life story, books, videos, workshops, events, and speaking to inspire others to follow their dreams despite their circumstances. Tanicia's theme for 2017 is "Purpose, Progress, and Moving Forward!" Tanicia looks forward to leaving an empowering legacy for her daughter, as well as enjoying the extraordinary journey that God has laid out for her!

Introduction

Approximately 2 years ago, I decided to create a book compilation. I had been featured in 2 book compilations prior as well as releasing my 1st book which is a semi-compilation. When I set out to do this, I really didn't know what to expect. I would say that's what some might call stepping out on faith or maybe even taking risks. To be honest, years ago I knew I wanted to write a book about dating and relationships but it was not on my priority list; however, I did write a few pages of it over 9 years ago. I wouldn't even call myself a "writer" because I never thought I was. When I think back, I think that was truly because I was still getting a full grasp on what my purpose was in life. I never thought much about purpose, but when it came to setting a goal to become the 1st person in my immediate family to graduate from college, I was determined to do that. After graduating college, when I reflect back, I still don't think I had a clue what so-called purpose was. I was not in church, but I had attended church here and there over the years; however, I never joined or got baptized. I can't tell you if I had faith or not. I knew I just lived, and I knew that I wanted to accomplish any and everything I put my mind to. You see, I was one of those kids who never truly had a "talent." I can't say I was great at sports, but I mean I was a cheerleader in 7th grade and did choir and dance in 11th grade. None of those things ignited a passion inside of me. I started a

Introduction

successful event planning and hosting Entertainment Company, planning and hosting several events from Sacramento to Pittsburg and beyond. I planned and hosted several amazing events from photo shoots to fashion shows to music showcases, etc. My entertainment company, *Cause N' A Stir*, is where I started to understand my passion for planning. I am great at it, but still, where does that word "purpose" come into play?

So even at age 30, I don't think I really understood the word "purpose," and I don't think I honestly gave it much serious thought. All I knew was I would do whatever it took to accomplish my goals, and failure wasn't an option. Fast forward, this is now my 4th book compilation project and now I feel a sense of purpose. The authors featured in the book compilations often thank me for all I have done for them, but I truly thank them for helping me discover my purpose. The amazing people I have been blessed to coach and work with have truly blessed my life. You see, helping others in turn helps yourself to discover purpose. This year has been an absolute rollercoaster which I will tell you more about in a later book. You see, today is August 14th, 2017, and in a month I will be having my 4th heart surgery. During this time in my life, self-evaluation is so important. I think of the scripture when God says "Be Still," and I know He is speaking to me. I know He is telling me and showing me to trust Him. As I mentioned

Introduction

earlier I was not in church before but that changed in 2015, and I was baptized in January 2016. I am faithfully in church now, every Sunday. I have dealt with so many things during my transition after my baptism. There are periods in your life where you think you have everything under control, but then there are those moments that make you question if that's true or not. Life can throw you so many curveballs with all the twists and turns. From never knowing what purpose was to seeing where my life is now, I can I know without a doubt that I have purpose. All that I have accomplished, but even more so being able to help/assist others during this journey, has shown me truly what purpose is. If you are ever stressed and you begin to question your life's purpose, remind yourself that everyone has a purpose in this world. Even if it takes some time to truly discover yours, be sure to live your life in the meantime. Also be sure to be in tune fully with yourself as to who you are because only YOU can define YOU. Lastly, if you don't take steps to make your dreams/passions a reality, you may never know your true purpose. Be bold, be brave, be fearless, live for you, be humble, and pursue happiness.

There are some things and quotes I want to leave you with:

- My pastor Shaun Nepstad said, "Everything you want in life is on the other side of a painful decision."

- "Every challenge I face is an opportunity for God to strengthen me." *Power Thoughts Devotional* by Joyce Meyers

- It's important to keep your mind in shape just as you would go to the gym to keep your body in shape. Just as you change your diet with what you feed yourself, it's also important to manage what you allow into your mind and thoughts. #MindsetRehab

I truly thank all the amazing authors in this book for deciding to keep working with me knowing I was having my 4th heart surgery during this book compilation. The faith they have in me as well as themselves shows me that God is working in all of our lives. Thank you all.

Discovering & Pursuing My Purpose

Elementary to High School

By

Holly Cranshaw

Author-Writer-State Licensed Aesthetician

Owner Red Carpet Skin Care/Goddess Cosmetics
Aspiring Life Experience Coach to Young
Teens/Motivator/Mortgage Loan Officer

What does the title of my chapter mean? Let's first discuss the meaning of "Purpose".

Pur-pose/noun/ the reason for which something is done or created or for which something exists (Webster's Dictionary). Pretty powerful if you stop to actually hear yourself read the definition.

When I was little, the words that came from my dad's mouth to my ears were always, "You have the potential to be anything you want to be". As I grew up, I still heard the words, but it was in the background, faint, almost muffled. I really liked school when I was little. I attended Lutheran Schools, ran track, was in the Girl Scouts and school plays, and it was fun. I did not know anything different until my parents bought their first home, moving us from Bernal Heights in San Francisco to Daly City, CA.

In the middle of the 5th grade, I had to transfer schools. I went from Lutheran School in the avenues of San Francisco to a public elementary school across the street from the house my parents purchased. I wore dresses because I did not know anything else. One day on the playground a girl walked over to me and asked me, why I talked the way I did and why I wore dresses every day. When I found out girls did not have to wear dresses every day, I was so excited. I remember going shopping that weekend to buy pants. I still enjoyed school but the kids were very mean. I would hide my pain with smiles and laughter. I needed an outlet and sports weren't working. I had all these emotions and "voices" talking in my head. Yes, I may sound crazy but we all have them, the loud thoughts, and the quiet whispers. I noticed that when I started writing, I felt a release and calmness. I enjoyed the calmness my spirit got when I would write.

Not having any "emotional support" I went from an A student to a C student, masking my sadness and not being understood with smiles and laughter. I still liked the learning aspect of high school, but hated going to school. After having my son at the age of 18, I did not know anything but to love and protect my son; that was my purpose in life AT AGE 18. I did not have a guide on how to be a mother but natural instincts are powerful.

You cannot be pregnant and live in my house; those words were gentle and stern at the same time. I remember my dad dropping me off at an all-girls group home/home for pregnant girls in San Francisco, CA. I can remember the look on his face as he checked me in, saw my room, gave his baby girl a hug and left. I felt alone and abandoned. I would just read every day to keep my mind occupied. It wasn't a good feeling. As a girl, you want your daddy's approval and my dad and I were very, very close. He was stern and gentle and at the same time...CRAZY. So, you could imagine there was a sense of disappointment on my end, but I was keeping my baby, Raymond. I had his name picked out when I was 5 months pregnant. My dad and my grandpa became the best foundation of MALE LOVE for my son. For two years we, my son and I, had a safe environment. The other girls were nice, we had chores and you got paid at the end of each week. The staff was nice and I was able to talk in group settings, gain a little of my self-confidence back, write, listen to the other girls and just be there for them and them for me. It was a no-judgment zone.

A few years later, we moved out of the group home but we still resided in San Francisco. I was working and my son was in kindergarten. I moved across the Bay to a home that my friend's mother owned. I was always drawn to administrative work, support roles, so I ended up working as an administrative assistant, and that was exciting. Having the support of a manager who looked like me was impressive, so I thought, and that would eventually be the reason I resigned. My manager and I were both single parents and she knew I had a small son. At that time, I did not have a car and my son was 4 or 5. I was arriving 5 minutes late to work every day, and after two weeks I got written up. I was disappointed because my manager knew what I had to go through just to get my son to his grandmother's house in Hayward CA. Dropping my son off at his grandmother's house on his father's side would become my worst nightmare as a single parent, and it was one of the reasons I resigned and took another position at a different company.

Since no one living in his grandmother's house would come or was able to come and get my son from the Hayward BART Station, I had no choice but to put my small child who was no older than 4 years old on the bus by himself so I could get to work and keep my job. Anyone who knew my son and his grandmother knew the LOVE they had for each other was unbreakable. (Rest in Peace Theresa Temporal) I was in tears and sick to my stomach that no support would EVER be given by my son's father, we will call him CT. (I threw that word EVER in since it's been 34 years.) The bus driver(s) knew us because I used to catch the bus, drop my son off and get back on the bus as it headed to the BART Station, but that did not make it any easier and I would cry all the way to work. It just destroyed me emotionally. There was a blind spot where he was supposed to get off the bus and he had to cross the street; each driver would make sure they dropped him off as the bus was heading down the street so he would not have to cross the street, and there was a lady who would watch my baby walk down the street each day until I was able to buy a car.

After all of that just to get to work on time, I got written up again. Y'all know if you miss that last BART train, the one that makes you RIGHT ON TIME, it's a wrap, you're late. Feeling like I had no support at work or in my personal life, I interviewed and got another job, excited to leave and start a new direction.

Relationships

You like a boy, he likes you, that's it, right? No, that's far from it. Few people are able to find and marry their high school sweetheart. It's the, "Aww we've been married for 50 years", but with those 50 years you can bet they went through the "getting to know you" phase for real!

When my fiancé and I moved in with one another, it was good, or what I perceived as good. We did everything as a family, we genuinely loved being around each other and we were friends. His family was amazing. I loved my new job, I was engaged, and I was moving forward with my life. My fiancé and I would talk once I got to work, it was our daily routine. One morning I decided to call him; car phones had just come out so you know he thought he was doing important things. Hello, she said Hi. I asked for my fiancé by name and she hung up. I go on about my day, he calls my job and I do not answer. Later that evening when he picks me up I say, I called you this morning, he says I called you back. No, I called you before 9am and some girl answered your car phone. I knew something was going on, but I like to have proof. So I left it alone, because one thing that I learned the hard way is, what is done in the dark, comes to the light.

A few weeks later I answer my work phone, and I ask how can I help you. It was the chick that my fiancé was seeing. Now, I was at work, so I had to keep my cool and I was only 23 so my first instinct was to slam the phone down, but I couldn't. I talked, asked questions and asked her to call me when he got there. Before I hung up I asked how she got my work phone number. He called me from her house one day when I paged him, so my work number was on her phone bill.

A few hours later, my phone rings and it's "HER". I hear her hand him the phone, saying it's for you. I said, hey, how are you? We will talk when I get home, I said bye and hung up. We stayed together two weeks after that incident, and then I moved out and got my own place, me and my son. What eventually ended the relationship was one day when I got out the shower; my ex-fiancé was sitting on my couch. I was startled, and he said never leave your back door open.

Now, to get to the back door you had to climb over the banister and it was not a small climb. I got dressed and he wanted to talk so I did, even though I was feeling very uncomfortable. After numerous questions and what seemed like hours, I repeated, I do not want to be with you. It was like I saw SATAN himself and he punched me in the thigh. Back then I wore dresses to work and shorts all the time, so that ended that for a while. Each day I looked at that bruise, which was the size of a cantaloupe, turn purple, then red, then black, and finally over a month it disappeared, just like he did. For at least two months after the incident he would send a dozen white roses to my job once a week until he finally got the point.

Discovering My Purpose

I moved myself and my son back to San Francisco for a while and then to Concord, CA. While living in San Francisco my skin would break out and I would start to get acne facials. I had a tough time following their prescribed regimen. These women were telling me what to do with my skin and what to use, however they did not look like me. So after a year, I enrolled in aesthetician school in Concord and became a State licensed aesthetician with a craving to work in a dermatologist's office to learn as much as I could about acne, skincare and products for ethnic skin. My son would come to the school because I needed someone to practice on. He seemed to be more excited than I was when I started my classes; I guess that is because I talked about it for so long. I was working two jobs and had to quit one when school started. I would work all day, go home and fix dinner, and then race to school. Luckily school was down the street and my son was just amazing and supportive at the age of 14.

I realized I was good at this, giving facials, consulting, and massages, and I actually loved what I did. I had people asking me for advice, which was new to me. I was appreciated.

I could not support myself and my son on an up and coming aesthetician's salary so I had to go back into the mortgage/real estate industry full time.

The one thing that was constant in my life was listening and being supportive. I was too willing to listen, too willing to guide, and I had nothing left for me. I had all these "ideals" and yearning for what I wanted in my life, yet it was easier to guide people to their destiny instead of listening and guiding myself toward my own. I knew I had something in me that was special, and in each position I held in the real estate/mortgage industry I thrived on helping people, giving them the information they needed, and I love skin care, the afterglow of my work and the excitement of my clients when they saw their skin and their commitment to come back and keep up their daily routine.

It's funny how we can talk ourselves out of the very place GOD is leading us to. Some people are more grounded in their vision and move towards it knowing that the rest will fall into place with no FEAR, just FAITH. It is so easy to second guess and doubt ourselves. Funny thing is, I wrote a book years ago called "Love and Consequences" along with a slew of poems, of which 3 were recorded to music. But with "Love and Consequences" only two people knew about it: my son and one of my good friends whom I've known since 1997. I never did anything with the book just because I did not know how to self-publish, but I was excited about it. I was in the bookstore one day and walked over to check out the new books and saw a book with the title that read "Love and Consequences". I felt a knot in my stomach and called my friend. His words to me were, when GOD gives you something and you do not use it, he will give it to someone else. That did not stop me from writing but it did make me pay close attention to GOD'S whispers. It has taken me a little while to get to this place of JUST knowing and seeing my vision of life. I asked myself, what would you do if you were successful by your own standards? And then I would smile and feel a calmness come over me. I have never had a lot of money, or material riches I could brag about like some people do. I did notice I had one thing, and it was constant and I kept going back to it…this thing called FAITH. I am slowly getting to know what FAITH is all about.

I had faith at 18 when I had my son, I had faith when I had to put my son on the bus, and I had faith when I was getting out of an abusive and destructive relationship.

Yes, we grew up in the church but I could not quote a scripture to you if I was hanging by one leg; well I guess that is a bit dramatic, but I can meditate and feel my energy getting stronger.

I am able to shut out, block out and rid people from my life now with ease. I used to feel guilty about doing that, but everyone does not wish you well and I did not understand that until I experienced it myself. Some people can take it when you are up but do not know what do when you have that one hand reaching for help, needing someone to pull you up like you have pulled them up. I have fallen more times than I can count, and sometimes it was due to nothing more than LIFE! I still cry, I still ask why, and with that I get more energy to move forward.

Talking myself out of being successful is a skill I used to have. It's different when you have a fear of failing, but all too often when asking myself WHY, the answer was could you have a fear of success? That could be as crippling as having a FEAR of failure and failure isn't a bad thing, at least you try.

I have learned the one thing you think about all the time as far as passion is what you should go after. When others see your light, one of two things will happen: they will encourage or they will disappear. Find a mentor, someone who you can trust if you need guidance in that certain field. Trust your instincts. We all have a gift; it's called intuition, some stronger than others. Learn how to listen to the whispers and find strength in whatever that is that gives you motivation.

I am just getting started, and what I want to say to young girls, and just people in general, is love yourself, encourage others, listen to the whispers before they become brick walls you walk into, and most of all, protect your energy and your light. Mistakes are a good thing, but not trying is giving into the negative and fear you hear inside your head.

My energy is drained

My spirit is gone

I'm in a state of unbalance

Like a see-saw with not enough weight on the end

Wavering

Venom is in the air

I swallow it as if it were brandy

It warms my soul, blocks my pain only to feel like a machete

Tearing a hole thru me

Not knowing it was pushing out the evil to bring in the sunshine

A breath to a new life

Original Written by Holly Cranshaw and published 12/15/10

About the Author
Holly Cranshaw

Holly Cranshaw was born in Portland Oregon and raised in San Francisco, CA. She is the youngest of three. She is a single mother of an amazing son, Raymond Anthony, and a grandmother to Sophya Isabella; these two are her heart and soul.

Holly always took solace in writing. With a natural ability to listen and guide, she got her AA in Psychology. After over 17 years in the real estate industry, she is on her way to getting her real estate license and opening her own real estate consulting firm.

In 2000, she became a state licensed aesthetician. She is a published author and was professionally interviewed in Skin Inc. Magazine in April 2001, the leading magazine in the beauty/esthetics industry. She will continue to grow her esthetics business with facial parties, in home spa facials and body wraps, educating women of color on skin care while continuing to fine-tune her own skincare and cosmetics line.

She has learned to stay positive, seek guidance and have faith. Things have not been easy but with each challenge she always sees the light. Until then, she will smile with laughter.

Holly is still figuring out her life and legacy, and in the process she needs to remember THE BEST IS YET TO COME!!!!!

When a train goes through a tunnel and it gets dark, you don't throw away the ticket and jump off. You sit there and trust the engineer. Trust GOD today no matter how dark your situation. GOD says, "You are coming out!" Quote RevRun via Instagram

Broken
To
Resilient

I Rise

By

Briggette Rockett, M.Ed.

(Brig-GETTE Rah-ket)

Author, Holistic Health, Lifestyle & Career Coach

Email: unmaskyourtruth@yahoo.com & bodyevolutionbe1@gmail.com

Website: www.unmaskyourtruth.com

It's was 6am Monday morning when I was told to get up and get a paper bag to pack my clothes, since I didn't want to be at home I was being dropped off at the Juvenile Center. WHAT?!! My heart dropped and began racing, I became scared, nervous, and wanted to throw-up, and tears were rolling down my cheeks. I wondered if I was dreaming, this had to be one of my bad dreams. I tried jerking myself awake, but it did not work, this was real, but it felt surreal. I began moving slowly, putting clothes in a bag, no comfort items like my toys or dolls, pictures, games or books, just clothes. I truly didn't know what was about to happen to me, whether this was temporary or a scare tactic. I wanted to ask but I was afraid to speak, so I did what I was told. The car ride was the longest of my life. As I looked out the window at the people going on their way to work and school I was wondering who else was going through a traumatic life experience right now. No words were spoken until we pulled up to a large building sitting on the corner and stopped. It was Juvenile Hall. "Go to room 123, and let them know you don't want to be at home anymore and someone will help you". In my head, I was screaming, I do want to be at home, I really do. I got out the car, no good byes, no hugs, and then my mother sped off to work. I stood there with my brown bag in hand, watching her drive away, and then I turned to look at the building. I was in shock. It didn't cross my mind to run away 'cause I could have, who would have stopped me? I could have gotten lost in the world, but I was scared and where would I go? No money, no one to trust and pregnant. Yes, I was 14 and pregnant. If that wasn't enough life alteration, now the loss of my home and the feelings of being abandoned added to the trajectory of my life. The sh*t just got real. As I walked into that cold, sterile building, looking for room 123, I came across the glass door and walked inside: "Can I help you", the woman asked.

In my soft low voice, "my mother told me to say 'I don't want to be at home'.

She asked, "What is your name?"

"Briggette Rockett."

"Yes, we have spoken with your mother. Have a seat over there; someone will be here shortly to pick you up."

Pick me up and take me where is what circled in my head. What was happening to me, what had I done so horribly wrong that I wasn't wanted anymore and we couldn't have worked this out or come up with a better solution than this? Well, during that time, I didn't get along with my mother; actually I hated her. Even though I had all the material things, nice clothes, piano, modeling, and dancing lessons, private school, nice home, food, and life was decent, for whatever reason there was a disconnect with her and I. I didn't feel she loved me during that time. I felt more love and warmth from my daddy then her. I remember not wanting to be at home, asking my favorite auntie and uncle if I could come live with them or wishing my best friend mother could be mine. There was some reason why I was feeling this way, but as a kid you don't understand these emotions, you just know they're there. Remember, I was a teenager and that was my truth then, and now I love my mother. It took getting to know myself, growth, maturity and psychology classes for me to understand, forgive and not blame her.

I admit, I was a very sensitive child, Michael Jackson like "Tito pass me a tissue" emotional, cried about everything. My mother being the authoritarian and aggressive personality that she was, our styles just clashed. I believed her to be too mean and strict. It was her way or no way. She was old school; a child was to do as they are told, period, with no talk back, no under the breath comments, and you had better cry in silence. These kids today know nothing about old school discipline, the type of training that instills values, morals and respect for your elders and others, and it would be your foundation for maneuvering through life. This is part of the reason some kids are running amok today because of not having that old school training, and this is where I may have failed my kids by being a little too liberal, but that's a topic for another day. At the time, I didn't understand her methods, all I knew was that I didn't want to be anything like her and I wasn't going to raise my kids on those strict teachings. Little did I know those strict teachings are sometimes necessary, because if you don't lay down the law and be consistent it can cause your kids a world of hurt in the bigger scheme of things, especially when they have to get out there and survive on their own. This world is a pretty harsh place, especially if you don't have the right foundation to navigate through it. Nevertheless, I used to wish she and my daddy would get a divorce because I would go with him. Once I even told one of my teachers she was my stepmother. I also hated when people said, "You look like your mother". I didn't see it then but oh, I see it now. For the most part I was an obedient child, a little stubborn, wanted my way, and spoiled but I never talked back to her, and I wasn't disrespectful. I did what she told me to do for the most part. She definitely had control, especially since I was scared of her, but I also wanted her approval that I felt I didn't receive. Nothing was ever good enough; no matter how hard I tried, she would find some sort of fault. Maybe that was the breakdown in having a bond with her, maybe she wanted me to be perfect, maybe she had an idea or image that I didn't match up to. Either way we both were looking for something from each other that wasn't being received. Her tone wasn't a very loving or supportive one to me especially since I was the sensitive type. I picked up on negativity easily so her aggressive tone didn't work well.

Becoming a teenager and being involved with a boy wasn't a good mix for our relationship; this is especially when everything went totally downhill for us. With having strict parents, being a girl and first born was the wrong combination because I wasn't allowed to do much of anything, which I guess created my sneaky behavior. I think anybody, especially a teen that doesn't have a good relationship with their parents, minimal communication and the inability to explore life and be trusted, would become sneaky, right? There is a saying, watch out for those quiet ones. Yes, that was true. I became sneaky. The loss of my virginity happened during the summer when my parents were at work and I was struck in the house every day for the whole summer doing nothing. Can you say curiosity killed the cat? This is why it's important to keep your kids active so they stay out of trouble, especially during the summer. The boy I chose to give myself to created havoc in my world. My first year of high school was a sham, F's, D's, 46 absences, 55 absences in all my classes to keep up with him. He had me going against my parents; it was like I was under some type of mind control or just stupidity at its finest. I just wanted to do what other teenagers were doing, hang out, especially with him. My high school was having a football game and I wanted to go. I asked my mother, and of course she said no. I devised a plan to run away from home so I could go to the game and be with him and thought after I came home I would be embraced with loving arms. They would be so worried about me, well, that is how the Latter Day Saints commercial went. See how that damn TV can mess up a child's head, particularly someone naïve?

By being told no, it made my plan easier to carry out. When I left for school in the morning I took some of my favorite clothes over to my auntie's house that lived over the hill from us and told them I was running away. Oh silly me. What causes such chaos and confusion in a teenager's mind? The hormonal changes teens go through is crazy. Their brains are being reshaped and reconstructed along with the addition of their current needs and experience. Well, my needs and lack of experience were differently driving the wheel on my choices and decisions. I didn't come home after school, I went to the game. He and I were standing and talking when I heard my name being called. It was my sister and my mother in the car. He grabbed my hand and we took off running. All I heard was my mother's car screaming into gear, but she didn't catch us. We ended up at his house in Daly City, and I called my best friend. Her mom talked me into going back home but I was scared, thinking about what my mother was going to do to me for creating all of this havoc. I knew she was hotter than a house on fire. As you can guess, my Latter Day Saints scenario didn't go as planned. My best friend's mom came and took me home. I just knew my mother was going to beat the living daylights out of me. To my surprise she didn't touch me, but I felt her anger so strong I could have sworn she was using her mind to suck the life out of me like Darth Vader. The tension was so thick I didn't want to breathe so I wouldn't draw any more attention to myself. My daddy had such a loving yet concerned look and tone, however my mother, if looks could kill, I would have died a thousand deaths. At this point, all I wanted to do was go to sleep.

Drama continued as I stayed in the relationship with this boy. Mind you, I was 14 and he was 15, and he was definitely more mature then the average boy. He physically abused me, burned me with cigarettes, hit me with wire hangers, handcuffed me to the bed and took me against my will, and he cheated on me with my best friend who lived next door to me. The time he burned me with cigarettes all over my body, I ended up running out of his room screaming, drunk and butt naked into his mother's room. How embarrassing! She had to find underclothes for me to put on, it was a crazy scene. There was also another night when I didn't come home. This time it wasn't intentional, he had me so drunk I couldn't get up in time to get home. My parents came to his house looking for me; they were in the living room talking with his mother while he had me hide in the closet. What comes to mind as I write this is the R. Kelly song, Trapped in the Closet. His mother came in the room looking around, and she looked in the closet. I could have sworn she looked right at me, but she left.

Now, after all of this, and this was only the beginning, I became pregnant. If I had only listened to my mother. She had found my diary were I indicated I was having sex, so she did what a parent was supposed to do: take me to get protection, some birth control pills. But because I was being defiant, I didn't take them. My senselessness would become a hell of a start to life and love.

My first instinct was not to go through with the pregnancy because I knew having a baby wouldn't be a walk in the park, but he wanted me to keep the baby so I followed his choice because I was so in love with a boy who I thought would have my back. I equated his abuse to love and had hopes of having a fairy tale life that I saw in cartoons and pictures. Wow, I was so inexperienced. I definitely watched too much television and it diluted my brain. I didn't tell my parents about the change in plans until an unpleasant conversation occurred with me and my mother. I blurted out, "Whether I keep the baby or not I don't want to live here anymore." Why did I say that to her? That was the wrong thing to say. Teenagers say things they don't always mean all the time, particularly in the heat of the moment and usually regret it later. Oh, how I regretted it. Yes, I used to say I wanted to live with someone else, I told friends and family members that, but I truly didn't understand what that meant, or how it would make me feel if it happened. The saying you truly don't miss something until its gone is so very, very true.

Now there I was, at Juvenile Hall, wanting to go home because of him and his decision and the magical words I uttered, "I don't want to live here anymore". Now, I was sorry for what I'd said, I was sorry for getting pregnant. I was sorry for causing trouble. I WAS SORRY!! My thoughts were spinning out of control and at this point, nothing was going to save me from the trajectory that had been mapped. As I sat and waited, it seemed like forever before a middle aged Caucasian woman appeared and asked, "Are you Briggette Rockett",

"Yes."

"I am Ms. Prechit, your social worker and I am here to take you to Florence Critten."

In my head I thought what is a social worker? What and where is Florence Critten and what is really happening to me? But my only response was "Okay." As we walked, my head hung down. The corridor seemed long, and it was cold and sterile. We went to the parking garage and got into her car. As I sat silently, scared out of my mind, Ms. Prechit asked if I understood what was happening. I answered, "no".

She began to explain: "You are being sent to a temporary group home called Florence Critten. It is a group home for girls, until St. Elizabeth, a home for unwed mothers, has a room available. You are currently a Ward of the State, meaning your parents no longer have legal guardianship over you. The facility you will live at and the courts will make all decisions on behalf of you and your child. You will remain in a group home until the age of 18, and at that time you are considered an adult and will be out on your own."

As she talked, tears started streaming down my face. As I stared out the window, my body became numb. All I heard was wah, wah, wah... We pulled up to Florence Critten and my heart began to race. I wondered if this was what it felt like to go to jail. We walked up to a red brick building with a black gate and a camera in front and a buzzer sounded. We walked in to be greeted by a woman with a pleasant smile. She would end up being a really good friend to me.

"Hi Briggette, I am Ellessee, I will get you settled in."

Ms. Prechit and Ellessee talked for a minute, then Ms. Prechit turned to me and said she would be in touch and left. My heart was pounding. Ellessee showed me around the facility, told me the rules and introduced me to some of the girls that were there being punished for not following the rules. The rest of the girls were on the weekly outing. Each night I cried. This wasn't what I envisioned for my life. I was going to graduate from high school, get a sports car, move to France, become a model, then get married have 6 children with a nice house, white picket fence, and take care of my husband and kids like the Brady Bunch. See, I told you my mind was brainwashed. Being a teenage mother is a very rigorous task. It takes strength, faith, intelligence, patience and family support. I knew nothing of what it took to be a good mother, I was just playing with dolls before all of these changes occurred in my life. I had no clue about life or myself, look at the choices I had already made. I wasn't grown by a long shot. I was a teen going through physical, emotional and mental changes. I was not even fully developed but now, instantly, I was considered an adult who had to live as an adolescent, if that wasn't conflicting enough. I believe parents, including myself, really don't understand the massive reconstruction that happens during adolescence. This time is unlike any other time in life. It is called sprouting, where the teenager's brain is reshaped and reconstructed. What a teen does and is exposed to during this critical time in life has a large influence on the teen's future, because experience and current needs shape the pruning and sprouting process in the brain. Being exposed to drugs, computer sex, or violent movies will also shape the brain and future of the adolescent, laying down the seeds of addiction and interpersonal conflict according to Psychology Today[1] Wow! Hindsight is 20/20. I had really messed up my

---

[1] Hedaya, J. Robert, M.D. "The Teenager's Brain." Psychology Today. 03 June 2010. https://www.psychologytoday.com/blog/health-matters/201006/the-teenagers-brain

whole reconstruction of my brain, as well as my kids that would come later.

Teenage pregnancy is the process of babies raising babies. They can barely provide for themselves or make informed decisions about their futures, but make the risky decision of engaging in sexual activities and making babies. Yet, I am here now and no matter how much wishing I was doing and the amount of tears falling I couldn't go back, my life path had begun. I was now in survivor mode with no clue what direction to take. I was not one of those fast learners, streetwise types of chicks. I was a straight Bambi, a deer in the highlights, so it was a one day at a time figuring it out as I go situation. I was making every mistake in the book while trying not to get ate by the wolves that preyed on the innocent, like my baby daddy, who would take your weakness and use it for his bidding. I was truly in a sink or swim situation. The group home only provided $5 a week for allowance and a $200 a year clothing allowance. Really! Even back then that wasn't enough to live on and with a baby too, it was crazy. My life of crime was about to start; well technically, it had already started because I use to steal money from my mother's purse when I was kid, and in high school I sold pinhead joints for $1, but those are stories for another day or when I complete my book UnMask Your Truth, now in the works. At Florence Critten, I was able to leave, but had to be back by 5pm or I would be on punishment, forfeiting rights to have visitors and not being allowed to leave for the weekend. I was okay with that so I spent a lot of time on punishment for not coming back on time or not at all. My attitude turned into an even more unhappy, angry, wayward teen that didn't care about anything anymore because I felt no one cared about me, except for him. He was the reason why I was in this situation in the first place, right? Or so I felt at the time, at least.

It was summertime and my belly was growing, and I had no clothes and barely any money. Growing up I was given the best of everything, spoiled and entitled, especially being the first-born, so of course I had a certain standard to what I was accustomed to. Earlier, I talked about the shaping of the brain and how experiences and exposure affect who you are; well my need to dress well was important and couldn't be ignored. This was one of the things I was exposed to. Did you think being in a group home was going to make me ignore my fashion sense? Nope. One day, on my pass, I was going to my baby daddy's house or his mother's house, and he wanted us to go to Serramonte Mall for me to steal some stuff for him. This would be my first time, and a skill not worth having because of the impact it would have on my daughter when she became a teenager, yet that's for another story too, maybe hers to tell. Again, the shaping of an impressionable brain with negative experiences and exposures is such a powerful truth. He would end up creating many first times for me that I shouldn't have been exposed to and this was definitely one of them. My experience becoming a thief was scary, but I did it because I was afraid of him and in love. Crazy, right? Beyoncé, Crazy in Love. Getting away with it was exciting and liberating, and it had now opened the flood gates of what was to come for my baby and me: clothes. The second time I went without him to Mervyns'. I walked in and left with a coat, shoes, and a purse stuffed with clothes. That was so easy. From that point on, I never worried about clothes again. I would look forward to the group home outings because they would take us to the mall, which would allow me to pick up maternity and baby clothes and other necessary items. What was I supposed to do? I couldn't get a job, and I didn't have any support, not even from him. So to me (a teenager), my actions were justifiable and it was about survival and doing what was necessary for me and my baby. The title of a known thief in the hood was "booster" and I became skilled. I never went to jail but was caught on several occasions. Lucky for me I had an uncle on the police force with the same last name. They would ask me if I had a brother or uncle on the force, and when I said yes they would call him and release me. I thank God for him; he saved my a*s many times. There were a few times I was in other counties boosting and where my uncle's name didn't hold weight, so I would start crying and praying, knowing this would be the time they would take me away, but with God's grace and mercy I would be released. It would stop me for a minute and then I would be right back out there.

Over the years, there would be many bullets, and I would dodge a few that could have taken my life. And even though navigating through my life has been no walk in the park, I've learned how to accept most of my mistakes. However, the one that weighs the heaviest on my heart are the mistakes I've made when it came to my kids. Everything I did was with them in mind. I wanted a different life for them; I wanted to be a different type of mother, loving, wholesome, and married with a stable household, like how I was brought up. But I failed in so many areas. Even when I thought I was doing the right thing, it wasn't right at all; but God had reign in my life and theirs. This allowed me to stand strong in the toughest of moments, especially when I wanted to give up. And for that, I am so grateful. I was once told I had no backbone, but I think my struggles have differently strengthened me and my backbone. I have risen above obstacles that should have taken me out and proven statistics wrong on the fatality rate of young teenage mothers. There has been a world of hurt that has entered my soul and it took a lot for me to navigate through it, but I am stronger and wiser for it. Never Should Have Made It, by Marvin Sapp, that is absolutely right. There were people planted in my life who tried to take me out with their toxins, even today, but...I rise. Today, I stand as a woman of strength, with integrity and wisdom, knowing God has given me the heart, backbone, grace and faith to push on despite all the attacks on my mind, body, and spirit. Even at this stage of my life, I am continuously learning and growing, not letting anything or anyone hold me back from allowing me to spread my wings and soar. On my journey of life, I have learned I am a fighter. No matter how many times you knock me down, I will get back up ready to go again. To my children, Taiesha, Dijon and Ronnie (RJ), my choices were always about trying to do my best for you, be it right or wrong. My love for each of you is insurmountable and I will always be there when you need me the most, so stay vigilant, determined and strong. Be a fighter. The only one that is stopping you from achieving what you want is you, so Rise Above.

About the Author
Briggette Rockett, M.Ed.

Briggette Rockett (Brig-GETTE Rah-ket) is a woman of faith, strength and a humanitarian. She believes in giving back and volunteers with various organizations. Currently she is a volunteer career coach at the San Francisco Public Library. Briggette is a mother of three children, two boys and one girl and has a grandson who she loves to pieces, along with a bonus daughter and granddaughter. Becoming pregnant at the age of 14 changed the trajectory of her life, and she ended living in a group home for unwed mothers until the age of 18. Faced with many obstacles and challenges that left her intimately knowing what it's like to face seemingly overwhelming odds, she managed to receive an A.S. from City College of San Francisco and an M.A. and B.A. from San Francisco State University, making her the first female in her family to accomplish these degrees. Briggette looks at learning as a lifelong exploration and believes continued personal growth is necessary. Briggette Rockett is a featured author in Broken into Brilliance, which was released in June 2017, and she is also a published poet. Currently, she works a full-time job and is working to establish her health and lifestyle coaching practice. Briggette is a Certified Holistic Health, Lifestyle and Career Coach, and she started her coaching practice, Unmask Your Truth and Body Evolution, where she works with a mature audience in preparing a reinvention map that empowers and up-levels the mind, body, and spirit in order to live the most authentic life possible. She aspires to inspire and her desire is to be a light of inspiration to others, letting people know that through your mess, you are still blessed. Briggette is a walking testimony that through blood, sweat, and tears, achieving your goals is possible. Lastly, she believes that without self-discipline success is impossible, and no matter how many times you fall, just fall forward.

If My Story Inspires One Person Then My Job is Done!

God Moments

By
Vanessa Oden

www.VanessaOden.com
Connect with Vanessa Magali Oden.
YouTube: Vanessa Oden
Twitter: @VanessaOden
Facebook: VanessaOdenShow
Pinterest: Vanessa Oden
Instagram: VanessaOdenShow

There are moments that are seared into us so deeply that they are etched across our memories and become indelible. There are moments that we experience God in such a tangible way that we literally feel the presence of God. Moments that our hearts burn inside of us, and we know without a shadow of a doubt that we have encountered the Divine. I call these God Moments, moments that are undoubtedly God ordained. Moments that are orchestrated by God for us to experience Him in a new way, to be encouraged beyond belief, or even to see a verifiable miracle in our midst. God Moments!

If we look, we may find them everywhere. But if we are not in tune with the Divine, we can and often do miss them. I invite you into this journey with me, as I share some God Moments that I have experienced. Will you join me? In the next few pages I am going to share three to four stories that really stand out to me as God Moments, moments where I felt that God was in the midst. I pray that you are inspired and encouraged by these selected stories

A Man on a Mission

One day in my town, I went to local pharmacy to get a charger. It was randomly closed due to a computer outage, so I went to another one. I went to buy the charger, and the lady said, "Oh, we do not have any more of the kind that you need.

I said, "Dear Lord please! I really need one." Seconds later, I kid you not; she glances over and sees a charger someone had put in a different spot. She said, "Wow! I thought we were completely out in the store. What is this doing here?" I immediately became happy and said, "Thank you Lord!" *Really* loud. Yep. I really needed one. A man in the aisle near me said amen! He was also amazed! He saw it with his own eyes also.

Next, I went to the checkout. I was in line behind an elderly gentleman. He took a really long time. Some others were impatient, and I know what it is to be in line and people be impatient. It is a terrible feeling, and I did not want to do that to anyone. Secondly, I understand sometimes older people need extra time. Also, sometimes they are lonely and may need to talk to someone.

I felt the Holy Spirit at that moment pressing the scripture Isaiah 61 on my heart. I noticed that and reflected on Jesus and all that scripture holds. I began to thank God quietly in my heart as I waited in line. I overheard the cashier saying, "Wow, that's so sad. I am so sorry to hear it." She said it several times. Then the transaction was done. He turned around to me and said, "I am sorry I took a long time and held up the line." I told him it was no problem, that I understood, and told him, "God bless you." He paused and said, "Thank you, I really need it." I said a quick short blessing as he walked out the door and finished my transaction.

The cashier in passing said that she knew them, and his wife had cancer. My heart was deeply moved. It was beyond me, though. It was more than that. I grabbed my bag and was going to my car. I saw him in the corner of my eye, and I felt God strongly nudging me to go over there and pray for him and his wife. When I stepped outside, I saw him outside by his car exactly where I envisioned him to be. I was truly amazed.

I went up to him and asked him if it was ok to pray for him and his wife. Now, I had not met this man before, and this was truly one of those undeniable God moments. He said ok, and that he would like it. So we prayed, and as we prayed I felt his hand on my shoulder and God was in our midst, we could feel it. It was electric! He gave me a hug and it was a pure hug of gratitude.

He had such kind eyes. I saw the light within. He told me about his wife, and that they had been married 67 years. He told me about her sickness and some details about their life. He was understandably very concerned about her. I asked him if they were Christians, and he said they were. We chatted about evangelism a bit.

He asked me how old I was, and then told me he was exactly 50 years older than me. He is 90. We got a kick out of that. He told me that in 1936, he was given a prayer card and gave his life to the Lord. He pulled a little pouch out of his back pocket. Inside he had little cards with the same prayer he was given that very day in 1936. He said it has been near to his heart all these years. He gave me a few, and asked me to give them out when I feel led. I had many scripture coins in my purse, and in my bag there were a few tracts and a wordless book. I gave him a few scripture coins and asked him to give me some cards. We got a kick out of that too.

He thanked me and I said, "It is God who led me to you." I told him I would continue to pray through March. That is what I felt led to do. He paused, looked at me and said, "I should have gone first." It was a sad moment. I acknowledged that it must be hard. I told him you never know what God can do, and to keep praying. He agreed. We went our separate ways. The image remained with me. God was still not done!

Fast forward.

Shortly after, less than an hour, I went to a local grocery store. I heard the music in there, and it happened to be of the era that this couple would have enjoyed. I thought of them, and then I felt the Lord strongly nudge me to pray for them. I did. As I was interceding for them in the freezer aisle, lo and behold, I saw him again! He passed me with his cart, and we were going in opposite directions. I stopped and told him that at that EXACT moment before I saw him, the Lord had impressed upon me to pray for his wife and for him. He smiled kindly and was grateful.

I believe in God Moments. I believe in the power of the Holy Spirit. God's Spirit brings people together, and powerfully. Every time someone met God in the Bible, we see that their lives were altered. Every time. This still happens to this day. When we encounter the Spirit of the Lord, there is an undeniable shaking that takes place. There is nothing to describe it. No words can articulate what the feeling is.

When we pray in faith for someone, the atmosphere is literally changed! We praise and pray and blessings come down. Wars are fought in the spiritual realm. Prayer is powerful. When we step out in faith to pray with fire for someone, there's something powerful in that.

A lot of times we may not talk to others based on what they look like. We may see them as a different religion, color, or socio-economic status and we may pause to give a "reason" why we cannot stop. This man was almost everything "opposite" of what I am. I am short, he is tall. He is white, I am brown. He is older, I am younger. He is thin, I am plus-sized. His hair straight, my hair curly... etc.

All of these "labels" and divisions that we make up as humans could have potentially kept us from praying together. But with the Spirit of God, none of that even matters or pertains. On the inside we are the same. We are all created in the image of God. We are all born the same way; we have the same inherent needs as humans. God can and will use people from every walk of life to minister to you and unite in some way.

When we come into contact with the POWER of God, what an undeniable, rich experience it is! There is no box big enough to hold God! The things He can do are limitless! I want you to embrace that term, LIMITLESS! God can do anything and everything God wants to. But isn't it beautiful that we can partake in but a glimpse of His Glory. He loves us and His love does not end. It is everlasting. He wants to have a relationship with us.

Sometimes in life you have a God Moment where you encounter God and you feel Him in a new way. Or for some people the first time! In those God moments, we can put a pin in those, pause and really say wow! WOW! You want to tell everyone! Write them down so you can reference them later.

The children of Israel had stones or monuments that they would set out every time the Lord did something big, and often they would place a stone at the place to remember where God did those specific things. See Joshua 4. These are times to pause and remember what God has done in the place that He has done it.

Nowadays, we do not set up actual piles of stones. Sometimes it is a mental stone or monument. Maybe it is a written one. Maybe something physical. A time to pause and reflect on what God has done.

The story about the road to Emmaus comes to mind. This is my marker to remember this feeling of this day. The whole account is found in Luke 24. Two disciples were on the road to Emmaus and encountered a "man" who they did not know was Jesus. They had a chat about the recent events that just transpired, then walked along the road with him. They did not recognize him.

Luke 24:30-32 NIV

"As they approached the village to which they were going, Jesus continued on as if he were going farther. But they urged him strongly, 'Stay with us, for it is nearly evening; the day is almost over.' So he went in to stay with them. When he was at the table with them, he took bread, gave thanks, broke it, and began to give it to them. Then their eyes were opened, and they recognized him, and he disappeared from their sight. They asked each other 'Were not our hearts burning within us while he talked with us on the road and opened the Scriptures to us?'"

There will be moments where our hearts will burn within us. We will feel God's presence strongly! Across all of Scripture we see these divine God moments where people come into contact with the Lord and their lives are touched. There are so many examples! Moses and his meeting God in a burning bush. Abraham and his dream and God's promise to him. Esther and her bravery and being in the right place and the right time. Jacob wrestling with an angel and getting his whole identity changed! David the shepherd boy growing up to be King! Saul getting knocked off his horse, getting his identity changed and becoming a defender of the faith!

These things happen even to us. Small God Moments and large God Moments! God is still moving! Still touching! Still transforming lives! When I think about these times, I am also thinking about the people who came before me and carved out a path when there was no path. God Moments where family has overcome many obstacles and God has sustained them the whole way. I want to share a God Moment about my family, and how my family went out on a limb to trust God and come from Puerto Rico to the Mainland.

Just recently I found out that my great-grandmother, who died years before I was born, was unable to read or write. She was born in Puerto Rico. Many girls at the time were not afforded the opportunity to go to school unless they were wealthy. My grandmother had a fourth-grade education. During my grandmother's time, girls could go to school to learn rudimentary essentials, but often had to stop around the third or fourth grade to help out with running the home.

When my grandmother grew up, she saw the poverty around her. She saw the lack of jobs, and she and my grandfather made a decision. They decided to make a change and leave their island and bring their little family to New York City where there were more jobs and a chance for a better life. They learned to speak English and looked for more opportunities. Although my grandmother did not have a formal education that went past fourth grade, she was an early advocate for her children.

My father had heart problems and was placed in a school where they would only make potholders in class for fear of exerting stress on his heart. My grandmother saw the light in him, and advocated for him to go to a better school. She wanted him to go to a school where he would be able to learn to the best of his ability.

During that time, my grandmother had a difficult time convincing the school that my father could attend due to racial tensions in the country. They told her they did not "accept Puerto Ricans." She advocated endlessly for him to attend and finally, the school allowed him to attend and study there. At this new school, my father came to life. He began to excel in math and science, and began to receive awards. He graduated with honors, and eventually went to college and became a civil engineer. My aunt became a public school teacher and earned two master's degrees. My uncle became an architect. I went to college and earned a B.A. and then an M.A. Sometimes I sit back and think about the legacy that my family has had and I am in awe. Here I am, with opportunities that my great-grandmother and family only dreamed about. I am a product of their dreams. These are more God Moments.

Very often, I sit in the quiet and ponder the vastness of God. I ponder the miracles of the Lord. As an evangelist, I have seen several miracles, signs, and wonders. I have had my faith strengthened and been touched deeply. I want to share two that especially stand out to me: The day I saw a withered woman walk, and the day I saw a boy who was mute, speak. Please join me as these two stories unfold.

Withered Woman Walked

I remember it as if it were yesterday. I was attending a prayer event and there was an elderly woman in a wheelchair. She had been unable to walk for a while and her family had brought her to a prayer service for prayer. As the ministry team began to pray, I began to pray fervently as well. While we were praying, someone was holding her hands and she began to stand.

A hush fell across the room, and everyone continued to pray. Her legs, atrophied from years of not walking, wobbled and she struggled to gain her footing. I looked up. Something big was happening. Everything about the atmosphere was different. I was witnessing a miracle in progress. She began to walk, slowly at first, with her feet gingerly touching the ground, and as she continued to do so, her steps got stronger and stronger and stronger. Her family wept tears of joy.

People began to cheer. Then with someone holding her hand and in tears themselves, she walked around the room and began to take small leaps of joy. The room erupted in praise to God, and we cheered and cried tears of joy. Every hair on my body practically stood on end. This was the real deal. I could tell because of how the anointing felt, and the reaction of the woman and her family, and how I witnessed her legs, feet and steps change right in front of us. I have been around many prayer meetings and saw a marked change with this one. This was a God Moment unlike any I have ever seen. I saw this with my own eyes.

The next God moment is equally as eye-opening. I saw it with my own eyes, and to this day I am in awe of the work of the Holy Spirit and continually amazed, even now! What would you do if you saw a boy who was mute talk? It was a moment unlike any other!

Mute Epileptic Boy

I have been a part of intercessory prayer teams, deliverance teams, evangelism teams, prayer teams and altar call teams. I am very sensitive in the Spirit and to the anointing of the Holy Spirit. Often, if I am sharing an evangelistic message I will sense an opening like a door opening and then I will sense the Lord saying, "Give the invitation now." When I do that, people usually make a decision for God and want to accept Jesus into their lives as their savior. The same thing happens during deliverance or altar call time. Sometimes, we will get someone who is afflicted or tormented by evil spirits. I have seen this happen many, many times. This particular afternoon we were in Mexico and there was a father and son there. The father had brought his son forward for prayer. When I asked him what he would like prayer for he said his boy had not spoken in weeks and had been having epileptic fits. I asked him when the last time he spoke was. Then man told me he had taken the boy to a witch and that was the last time he had spoken. We began to pray for the boy and he could not talk. Then suddenly we felt a lift in the atmosphere. He raised his hands and said in Spanish, "Jesus is Lord."

Brothers and sisters, there are so many more that I could write of, things I have seen and have experienced. Times where God has shown Glory beyond anything that we could describe. I invite you, no matter where you are in your spiritual walk or on your journey in faith to dig a little deeper, dive a little deeper. Experience and embrace even just a little more. Let us take a moment to pause and ask ourselves and reflect as to where these God Moments are.

These God Moments are everywhere. When we take the time to open our physical and spiritual eyes we can start to notice times where God's spirit is moving and where God is showing his Glory. These God Moments leave us with a sense that God was in our midst and that God is with us along every step in our journey. Take time to look for the God Moments in your life, and share them as a testimony to those you encounter along your journey. You never know what spark you light in them. In doing so you just might make a lasting positive change, and if you have inspired just one, you have started a positive chain reaction that could potentially inspire and change the world!

My Prayer for You

I would like to pray for you, dear reader!

Lord, I thank you for each person reading this. Let us feel our hearts burning within us when we feel your presence. Blow upon us fresh, Lord God! Father, open the window of heaven and pour out blessings upon us that we do not even have room enough to receive. Wherever there is a sickness, Lord we pray for healing: mind, body, and spirit. Father where there are those hurting, we pray you bind up their wounds.

Provide Lord God for those who are in need. Lord you know our goings and our comings. Be with us wherever we go. Be with us in our homes, on our jobs, help us be shining lights. Help us to see you in the little things. Revive those who may be experiencing dryness, be with those who are asking for direction, and be with those who are seeking a Word from you. Lord, we thank you for who you are. We thank you that we can experience your Glory afresh and anew and experience these God moments in our lives.

In the name of the Lord, this is my prayer. Amen.

Many blessings,

Vanessa Oden

About the Author
Vanessa Oden

Vanessa Magali Oden is a true renaissance woman. She is a wife, mother, educator, minister, blogger, multi-passionate entrepreneur, radio personality, and community influencer. Vanessa was born in Brooklyn, New York, and was the first person in her family to be born on the U.S. mainland. She holds a B.A. in Pastoral Studies from Patten University where she graduated magna cum laude. She also holds an M.A. degree in Education with an emphasis in Educational Leadership. She is active in her community and serves on the Board of Directors of F.I.R.E. Ministries. She is an international evangelist, and also serves in her local ministry in a variety of capacities. She is a seminary instructor in Fairfield, CA, and a classroom teacher in the highest achieving charter school in Oakland. She also served as a commissioner of her local Parks and Recreation Committee in Williams, CA. Vanessa has traveled to over twelve countries on four continents. She loves to spend time in nature and enjoy her family. She is a mom of five children, and dedicates this book chapter to her entire family and friends, that they may always remember the "God Moments." Vanessa lives with her family in the San Francisco Bay Area of California. Vanessa hopes that her book will inspire others to see "God Moments" in all areas of their lives, and that they will be encouraged to soar to new heights.

You can read more about Vanessa on her website at www.VanessaOden.com.

My Mess Turned Into My MESSage

Walk of Worship

By

Benjamin L. Rivera

IT Application Support, Worship Leader, Musician, Real Estate Investor, Entrepreneur, Director of non-profit Reaching Down, and driven by the creative process.

Email: benlrivera@yahoo.com

Suisun, CA

Hello,

My name is Ben Rivera and this is my testimony of how my walk with God went from not wanting a thing to do with him or church, to how He opened my heart with a love for music and drew me closer to Him with an invitation to be on a worship team at my church.

God has taken me as I am and used my brokenness. This new and ever changing relationship is breaking down my walls and healing some of life's wounds.

When you go for a walk, there are many paths, hills, valleys, and decisions to make of people and situations in your life that will change you forever. Here are some of mine.

I was raised Catholic and for a short while went to Saint Margaret's Catholic School in Reading, PA for elementary school. While there I took some piano lessons and was in the choir. That was my intro into playing and performing music, but like most young kids, I did not like to practice. Playing with my cousins was way more fun. My mom enjoyed music and wanted me to have that also. Continued encouragement would keep music in my life with piano lessons at school and private lessons with Mrs. Elmer. Mrs. Elmer was an older lady in a big house with a lot of history in it that had pictures with untold stories. Every piece in her home was part of a collection of memories from her life. Now it seemed it was just her and her music. Since my cousin took lessons from her, my mom wanted us to take lessons from her as well. She was an old school piano teacher. Her style was strict and excellence was her goal for every student she taught. I would get nervous taking lessons because she knew immediately if I made a mistake. But you know what? She must have done something right, because I still remember those lessons and I think they helped me to be the musician I am today. I will forever be grateful for her teachings and my mom for taking me there.

Life always has a way of surprising us, and I was unaware that a big change was coming. My parents were going through a divorce and my mom was losing her job and in search of a new one. She took a teaching opportunity in Key West, FL. It was time to leave my home town and my family which I was very close to. Time to take on a new adventure. I have to admire the spirit of my mother. In spite of being a newly single mother with two young boys, my brother less than a year old and myself around nine, she hired a moving truck, packed up our car, and we left home to a new place. My grandmom accompanied us, which I appreciated. I loved any time I could get with my grandmom. She was the matriarch of the family and ruled with an unselfish love. Adrianna Adames was her name, and she was a huge part of my life. Born in Puerto Rico, she was married at a young age and brought to the United States when her husband, my grandfather, found work.

They settled in Reading, PA and raised their family. From some of the stories I've heard, it was not easy raising five kids in a new place, not to mention a different language. But she did it and learned how to speak English. A true testament to her courage and strength. She will always have a place in my heart. I love and miss her very much, as she has gone to be with the Lord.

We only stayed in Key West for one year before we packed up again and moved to Delaware. I don't know the reason for our move, but I would guess being so far from family was hard. Before leaving for Florida my mom had bought a vacation home (mobile home) in a park called Pots Nets in Long Neck Delaware, not far from Rehoboth Beach. We were there for a couple years and I really had a great time living there. I remember summers at the pool every day and hanging out with my friends. The beach was close and my mom loved the beach. We would go as much as possible. Music was there too, but in a different way. Now it switched to more listening and dancing. I started to really enjoy it. I would go to school dances and really caught on quick to the current dances.

My mom was a substitute teacher and was having a hard time getting a full time position. So we were off to the next adventure and path. She found a job in Maryland right outside of Baltimore. We again packed up and made the trek to yet another new place, leaving another home and friends. I don't ever remember being sad about that. I must have that same adventurous spirit that my mom has.

Time to start over again, new school, new friends, and a new home. We moved into an apartment called Twin Coves. There were a lot of kids in the apartments and in the surrounding neighborhoods. Music again was a big part of life for me. This was the early 80's and break dancing was getting popular. Movies like Breakin' and Beat Street were out and they inspired me and other local kids to learn this style of dancing. We would find sheets of card board and practice our moves. I also started learning a graffiti style of drawing. I had a friend named Dean that had some great techniques and I would learn from him. He also was into dancing. I would do a lot of drawing for the kids at school and then got asked by the school to do a mural on the cafeteria wall. This was for Marley Middle School. I think back now on how crazy that was and really an honor. I ended up painting in graffiti style, a horse character spray painting the name of the school on the wall.

One day I was hanging at a friend's house and we were watching a movie called Purple Rain. It was a movie about this musician called Prince. This movie blew me away!!! His charisma and ability to play the guitar really inspired me. After watching that movie I wanted to play guitar. That reality did not come for a couple of years. Now moving on to high school, we used to have off-campus lunches. I would walk to the mall down the street because they had a music store. I would go there and just look at all the guitars, remembering that I really wanted one but did not have the money to buy it. So an idea came to me. My mom would give me lunch money. If I did not eat lunch and saved the money, I eventually could buy the guitar. There it was the plan. I did not tell anyone that this is what I was doing. I just did it. Day after day, not eating a lunch got me closer to my goal of saving enough for my first guitar. After months of saving the day came. I finally had enough to buy the guitar and a small amp. It was the cheapest one I could afford and I think I walked out the door spending a little over a hundred dollars. Now I have this guitar and had no idea how to play it. After doing some research and learning that the notes are like the piano, I decided to paint the neck white and all the places that were the sharp\flat notes I painted black. Now it made sense because of my piano background. Thinking back now, this was a life changing moment for me. This was the moment music really was going to change me forever. The goal to learn this instrument became forethought in my mind. The people I would meet because of this decision to save my lunch money and buy a guitar would continue to inspire me and eventually develop my relationship with God.

I met this guy in school, Kenny Manny. He was a funny, heavy set, heavy metal guitar player. Not your normal visual of a heavy metal guitar player. He had a great ear for music but did not know music theory. I on the other hand did not have a good ear for music but did understand a little music theory. So this was the deal: I would teach him music theory and he would teach me how to play the guitar. What a great deal! I was just amazed at how he could learn songs by ear. He would crack me up with how excited he would get when he played. He would really rock out. There were many days that we would hang out at each other's houses, developing a friendship and playing music together. There were many other people I would meet through music and each one shared their gift and passion for music with me.

As I was getting older my willingness to go to church decreased. My faith in believing in God was diminishing. I have this thing called life figured out, why did I need this God stuff? That was my thought. So as a teenager getting ready to graduate high school and go off to college, I was alone. No God, no parents, and not living with family for the first time. I ended up going to Kutztown University in Pennsylvania. This is the school my mom went to. I was going to really dive into this music thing at college. I was excited for this, yet another new place, with new people to meet. As it turns out, I was in way over my head. I felt like I was so behind the other students. I had so much to learn just to catch up. Scared that I would waste my mom's money, not confident in my abilities, not willing to really put the work in, I sadly quit college after only one semester. I was taking a class and the instructor said some of you are not supposed to be here. I felt like he was taking to me. That was the moment I made the decision. I'm sure my decision did not make my mom happy. I ended up moving back home and then an opportunity came my way. I got a chance to work for PRS guitars. They were a top-of-the-line handmade guitar company that was based out of Annapolis, MD. Again music infused my life. I was there for about two years, and even though it was an amazing job learning the art of guitar building and meeting some of the current guitar heroes of the time, I just did not see myself working in a factory for the rest of my life.

A couple of years before, I was sitting in the kitchen with my mom when I told her I needed to go. She said where? I said I don't know. I just had the feeling I needed to go. Then a couple years later I made a decision and did not tell anyone after hearing stories from my mom's boyfriend at the time about his time in Vietnam when he was in the Army. He would say how the Air Force seemed to have it really good; while they were in the jungle the Air Force guys were in their barracks, playing volley ball and having BBQs. I was single, had no commitments, and was working in a factory. Why not check this Air Force thing out and maybe I could go see the world. So I did just that. I joined. It wasn't till a couple days before I was going to leave that I told my parents. It was a shock to them and my little brother. At the time I did not realize how much. My brother and I were close, and without warning I was gone. But when you are young you don't think of life that way. You are just thinking what is my path, what am I supposed to be doing? Again, off to a new place and new people.

After basic training and tech school I ended up at Travis AFB in California. I got my dorm room and had my musical instruments with me. I started feeling an issue with music. I wanted to be creative and make music but I was still immature in my understanding of music. I would get upset because I did not know what to do or to get the ideas in my head out. So I would have to cover my instruments because I would be so frustrated. I eventually made musician friends and would play with them, but still felt stuck in a rut musically.

Now for the next wonderful and big moment in my life. I met this girl, Julie. We got along very well and started dating. I got reassigned to Alaska with the Air Force. She eventually came with me. We got an apartment off base and were doing life together. Still young in the relationship and really one of my first serious relationships, I was determined that this was the person for me. I asked her to marry me. She had two kids from a previous marriage and we had a son together. Life got real and it was time to grow up, raise, and support a family. Music slowly made its way to the back burner. I still played from time to time but not like I used to. I started learning about computers and was thinking that would be my next career once I got out of the Air Force. Once I was out I immediately started going to school for just that, and also got my first job in computers. Going to school and working at the same time really elevated my learning.

As in most relationships we had our ups and downs. After fourteen years the downs were more than the ups. We both did damage. We both hurt each other. So then we filed for divorce. That was one of the hardest times in my life. I did not know what to do. I had no answers. I was hurt and angry and just really wanted to run away. But I could not do that. I was a father. I was responsible for lives other than myself. I had to suck it up. I had some good friends that really helped me talk things out.

After several failed relationships one lady I was dating suggested we go to church. I did not want to but I knew I needed to do something different because I was not doing any good on my own. We tried a couple churches and then went to a church called New Life. It's funny because I did not think about it then, but it was a place for New Life. We went with my son and we were both pissy being there. But I am the father and I had to be an adult. My son was sitting next to me, arms crossed and not wanting to be there. Inside I was feeling the same way. Ok, be the adult, be the parent, step above how you feel and what you want and be open for your son is what I was thinking. The band was rockin', electric guitars and modern sounding music. I turned to my son and said the music is good right? We both liked music and I knew if he focused on the music it would be easier. I saw his arms loosen. This was a big moment for both of us. Not only was the music good but the message that day was reflected the week I just had. Ok that is weird. So we decided to try this church again. The next time we came back they remembered our names. Weird!! The message again was relevant to what happened that week. Are these people following me around? Crazy, right?!!! So we started going regularly. It must have been the end of the year that they had some cards passed out for us to write our New Year's resolutions on it. One of the things I wrote on there was to be on the worship team. Granted, at that time my guitar skills were very rusty and I had not played with any sort of band in years. So I turned in my card and then went to talk to the worship leader. He said that the worship team practiced on Thursday nights and I was invited to come and watch. I did just that for the next four months. I had not ever heard these songs before and was not very good at playing with a band, but I did not give up. I showed up week after week, willing to learn. Then one day after practice he asked me if I wanted to play the next Sunday. I gladly accepted. Even then I didn't believe God was working in my life. I was doing it on my own. I was still struggling with my faith in God or even believing in God. Here I was, in church, struggling to believe, and on the worship team. This is one patient God to take me as I am and slowly use music to build my relationship with him. So slowly but surely God and I started having a relationship. I can't tell you the day or when it happened, but it did happen. Through worship God became part of my life. As I look back on this story and the different turns, ups, downs, and just defiance, God has been there. He has put people in my life, whispered ideas, and used my passions for His glory. This is the God I love. The God of relationship, who desires us to be in relationship with Him. Who with an open heart will use us as we are and change the world for someone we didn't even know. So I challenge you, find your passion, give it to God, and He will give it back to you more than you could ever imagine. This story is just a small glimpse of God's work in my life and the story continues every day. I just needed to work harder at allowing myself to be open and vulnerable to God's will, no matter how scary it is.

About the Author
Benjamin L. Rivera

Ben Rivera is artistically creative and enjoys surrounding himself with intelligent, talented people who have the desire to bring joy and new awareness to the world around them through their art.

Born in the inner city of Reading Pennsylvania, Ben spent much of his childhood moving around with his mother and brother from Key West, FL to Long Neck, DE then on to Glen Burnie, MD where he graduated high school. After high school Ben moved to Kutztown, PA, completing a semester of college at **Kutztown University** when he felt college wasn't for him and traveled back to Glen Burnie. He took a job with PRS Guitars, helping to work their first CE model guitar as well as one of their first guitar amplifiers. After two years with PRS Ben decided a change was needed in his life and he joined the United States Air Force, giving him the opportunity to travel once again. His time in the service took him around the world to 7 different duty stations, ending his military career at Travis AFB where he settled down in nearby Suisun City, CA. Being exposed to so many different places and people opened his mind to the endless wonder and possibilities of what the world had to offer.

Ben is grateful to the military for teaching him to have a purpose for studying and achieving goals, a teaching he has applied to everything that he has and still wishes to accomplish. His education is both formal and personal, learning everything from computer science to the art of music and dance as well as building relationships. To this day education is dear to him, with articles on the internet and audio books being some of his favorite ways to learn. Ben's favorite quote in life is "Life begins at the end of your comfort zone". That is a motto he continues to live by, always learning and trying new things that challenge him simply for the growth, joy and adventure of the accomplishment.

Today Ben is a father of three amazing children, two sons age 31 and 22 along with a daughter who is 28, and he still enjoys the arts of music, dancing, drawing and writing.

"The Beginning of a Destiny Begins With Tearing Down"

By
Dannielle Hart
Blogger/Author/Entrepreneur
Antioch, CA

www.hartwords.com
Facebook: God's Hart
Instagram: @hartwords
Social Media hashtags: #hartwords #godshart
Email: Danniellehrt@gmail.com
Hartwordsblog@gmail.com

"The Beginning of a Destiny Begins With Tearing Down"

"Yet if you devote your heart to him and stretch out your hands to him, if you put away the sin that is in your hand and allow no evil to dwell in your tent, then, free of fault, you will lift up your face; you will stand firm and without fear. You will surely forget your trouble, recalling it only as waters gone by. Life will be brighter than noonday, and darkness will become like morning. You will be secure, because there is hope; you will look about you and take your rest in safety. You will lie down, with no one to make you afraid, and many will court your favor" (Job 11:13-19 KJV).

From the beginning I grew up in an ideal town with ideal parents. My mother was very devoted to God and her family. My father was a minister and became a pastor. Both of my parents taught us right from wrong and did their Godly best to steer my siblings and I in the right direction. I was never a horrible child, but I think like most children and adolescents, I was stubborn. Once I got to be about eleven or twelve my attitude began to change and I became totally selfish and a know-it-all. During my adolescent years there was plenty of peer pressure to do all types of things from drugs to sex. At times it seemed that the more bad things you were involved in the more popular you were. If you weren't doing something a little on the wild side you were probably one of those kids who hung out by themselves in the back of the school or library during lunch. When the high school years start, those pressures become almost insurmountable if you are not rooted and grounded in the word of God and have a strong support system. At times even if you have these things you may still get involved with something that may affect you for the rest of your life. Even though I did get involved with people and bad habits that weren't the best for me, God was able to turn it around for my good. He saw the gifts that He had placed inside of me, and by me submitting to Him, those gifts are now able to develop and shine through. I did not allow my bad decisions to determine the outcome of my future.

Things change very fast, for the worst or for the better. When I was seventeen I decided that I wanted a boyfriend. At that age you do not necessarily make the best life decisions. Since I was an impulsive personality and tended to go after things that I wanted, I went out and got one. Not the best guy, but I achieved my goal: I got a boyfriend. I became sexually active and two years later I had a child, welcome single-motherhood. The goals that I had set for myself before pregnancy, in my mind, seemed to be slipping through my fingers at a breakneck speed. When you are so focused on the things God has not intended for you in the first place, those things rapidly take all of your energy to maintain. As I write I think of this scripture, Proverbs 16:9 MSG: "We plan the way we want to live but GOD makes us able to live it." Not saying life does not have its difficulties being a Christian, but you have a hope that things will get better if you are living within the will of God. At

"The Beginning of a Destiny Begins With Tearing Down"

that time I was not living within His will and the way He had planned for me. I was making plans but they did not align with the plan God wanted me to make for my life, so He could not establish me, He could not make me able or help me live those ill-thought out plans. I was in fact making things harder and more difficult for myself, but I am so blessed that I had and have a SAVIOR, Christ, who I can turn to in difficult times. He did not come to condemn the world but to save it and give us the promise of eternal life (see John 3:17). I am so glad that He did not condemn me or give up on me and allow me to continue making bad decisions and wallow in them. After realizing that I wasn't living at my best, it still took me some time to really learn and make a commitment to God's plan for my life.

When I became pregnant, I was very alone. Even though I was with the person I became pregnant by, there was still a lot of mistrust and stagnancy in our on and off again relationship. I knew that our union would never grow or last. God was definitely not first and it showed. Right before I gave birth to my child I prayed and cried out to God. I was at a point where I knew that things would not get better if I did not commit my ways to Him. My boyfriend was not faithful and I was not where I wanted to be in life. I understood why God wanted us to save sex for marriage at that very moment. With sex you create this physical and spiritual bond, a contract, which is very deep and is difficult to break. It's a covenant between you and that other person that seals and cements the relationship you have already created. You tend to realize a lot of things when you are in a horrible situation. When I sincerely cried out to God and asked Him to give me a scripture that I could carry with me, I opened my Bible to Isaiah chapter 54. The scripture we are familiar with is the very last verse which reads, "No weapon that is formed against thee shall prosper..." (Isaiah 54:17 KJV). As I read that entire chapter, the Holy Spirit began illuminating certain verses throughout. Some of the main verses that stuck out to me were, "For thy Maker is thine Husband..." (Isaiah 54:5 KJV), and "For The Lord hath called thee as a woman forsaken and grieved in spirit, and a wife of youth, when thou wast refused, saith thy God. For a small moment have I forsaken thee; but with great mercies will I gather thee. In a little wrath I hid my face from thee for a moment, but with everlasting kindness will I have mercy on thee, saith the Lord thy Redeemer" (Isaiah 54:6-8 KJV). Also Isaiah 54:13 KJV, which reads, "And all thy children shall be taught of the Lord; and great shall be the peace of thy children." These verses I carry with me even to this day to remember what God had said to me. Through my pain I was able to see God. I was able to see that He was concerned about me. Even though I had made a very wrong turn and got off course, His desire was to see me come out of my present circumstances.

"The Beginning of a Destiny Begins With Tearing Down"

At this point things started to change. I soon had my child but her father and I had not yet truly parted ways. I started to go back to church and I began college while caring for an infant. I went into every day thinking about those scriptures I was given and having hope that things would eventually get better. I was given an opportunity to go to an out of state university, so I did. As I said before, I was impulsive and a risk taker, so if it was a challenge I would go for it. This time I had learned that I needed to pray and seek God before making major moves. As I prayed I received a "yes" to go from the Holy Spirit and confirmation through scripture, so I leapt at the opportunity. Everything fell into place, and although my family wasn't too thrilled, I still went, excited about the new opportunities that were ahead of me. Side note: I have learned this through that situation: just because God says "yes" to you doing something doesn't mean that it will be a bed of roses. He might be leading you into a stretching and trying season. Sometimes these situations are learning and preparing times and I absolutely realized that with this move. So I moved all the way across country to an unfamiliar place with unfamiliar faces. I faced some very uncomfortable times there but God showed me extreme favor with people and I made some great friends. When it was all said and done I graduated college and after about 3 years of being there, for once and for all, broke up with my child's father. My Heavenly Father had used that time to show me who He was and who He wanted me to be at that time. God was able to isolate me in order to help me learn more about myself and to break me of some bad habits and ideas that I had developed that hindered His movement in my life. Me still living in a life where I was cheated on, lied to, disrespected, and not honoring my body (the temple of the Holy Spirit) was absolutely not His will or calling for my life. He had to change these things so that I could live according to His plan and have it stick. He was breaking up the old foundation I had formed my misshapen reality on in order to build a new foundation that He could properly build upon. He took from me the old to make room for His new. I keep a journal and on 7/26/2010 this is what God had revealed to me about why I was in the spiritual and physical place I was at that time:

Journal entry based on Hebrews 11:10 KJV and Psalm 118:22 KJV.

The Lord's Message to Me:

"For [Abraham] looked for a city which hath foundations, whose builder and Maker is God" (Hebrews 11:10 KJV). This is what God has sent me here for, that the things in my life would have foundations made by Him.

- My relationships
- Career

"The Beginning of a Destiny Begins With Tearing Down"

- Future marriage

- Ministry

- He is rocking the old foundations and forming new ones. He is making big holes like a jack hammer in the old foundation.

- "The stone which the builders refused has become the headstone of the corner" (Psalm 118:22). The old foundation wasn't suitable for what is to come. It would not hold the new structure that I [the Lord] am building.

The tearing up of my former foundation began with my break up: "Blessed is the one whom God corrects; so do not despise the discipline of the Almighty. For He wounds, but He also binds up; He injures, but his hands also heal. From six calamities he will rescue you; in seven no harm will touch you" (Job 5:17-19 KJV).

After I broke up with my child's father I had to reevaluate where I was going, who I was and what I stood for. What was I truly made for? How could I catch hold of my destiny? These questions popped up in my mind and for the first time, even before I stepped into this haze of disobedience towards God, I seriously had to face true growing up. I realized I wanted more for myself and that I was capable of achieving more. I had to be an example for my child. I could not live in a way that I would not be proud of her living. Through this self-examination

God was helping me to dig deeper and understand that I could do nothing really worthwhile without Him (see John 15). God is so good in all of His mercy. Even though I had walked away from Him, He still picked me up and pointed me in the right direction. After all the pain and hardship of living away from my home state, I moved back home. I was still broken yet healing and seeing life in a whole new way. Going from being in an on and off relationship with one person from my teenage years all the way into my late 20s was difficult to process. At this time I was in a huge transition process, now truly realizing that the father of my child would no longer be a focal point of our lives. I was also finding myself and a job after college, and adjusting to everyday single-motherhood. During this time God began teaching me techniques to stay focused on Him and be patient in the process.

Worshipping in the process is a very important. Everything that you do, including raising your hands in praise, is a form of worship towards God because He enables you to do it, so when you do things to the best of your ability He is glorified in those things: "So whatever you eat or drink, or whatever you do, do all to the glory of God" (1 Corinthians 10:31 ESV). I was and still am in an active growing period. I still dated men I should not have dated, still did things I should not have done, and trust me, I suffered consequences for those actions, but God still hung in there with me. The consequences helped me to stay in the right direction. Along the way God revealed things through dreams, scripture, prayer, etc. He has sent people to me with encouraging words and great mentors. A very hard lesson that I had to learn was how to stop having sex (fornicating): "Flee from sexual immorality. Every other sin a person commits is outside the body, but the sexually immoral person sins against his own body. Or do you not know that your body is a temple of the Holy Spirit within you, whom you have from God? You are not your own, for you were bought with a price. So glorify God in your body" (1 Corinthians 6:18-20 ESV). This is a hard subject but it is vital for a successful Christian walk. If you do not know what fornication means, let me give you the definition: it is having sex with someone whom you are not married to. I was never tempted to cohabitate with a man, but sex was an entirely different story. I had to come to the point where I would allow God to take that habit away from me. It took some time but after several failed attempts at dating and a broken heart, I was ready. I understood that through my disobedience and stubbornness I had blocked the flow of God in my life. He wanted more from me and I had to do some further releasing of ugly habits. God was able to use my horrible break up, failed dating attempts and other consequences to shape me and remove things that did not fit His program for my life.

Sometimes it takes years to find your way. Some people learn faster than others according to our standards, but God knows our individual learning curves. He knows what makes us tick and what we will respond to. In order for a person to change there is always a series of events that occurs that culminates into a reversal of attitudes and ideals that effect how they respond to their surroundings. Since their mind is changed about things, they will not respond to certain circumstances the same way again, thus giving them a different result, and hopefully helping them to turn their lives around for the better. I had to come to the point where I would seek out God and His answers for my situation. I was totally surrendered and knocking, yearning for God's wisdom for my life. For me it was fornication, but for someone else it may be drugs, alcohol, even gossiping, speaking negatively, etc. Anything that has an unnatural hold on your mind and body that halts your effectiveness in God's kingdom needs to be released to Him through the power of the Blood of Jesus Christ. In order for me to fully be delivered from the desire to have sex with men who I was not married to, I prayed a prayer of deliverance.

Prayer is powerful. In the Bible, the Apostle Paul talks about praying without ceasing (1 Thessalonians 5:17 KJV). That is truly important for a person's success in everyday life. I had to commit my way to Him, so that I would see what destiny He had in store for me. I had to align myself with His will, so that way when I make plans they line up with Him. If I was totally out of touch with what He was about I could not move forward. I would continue circling the same mountain, watching my life pass, unfulfilled, and hopeless. God showed me that I would not reach where He wanted me to go if sexual immorality continued to be present in my life. At first when you are faced with a decision to make, you make excuses and drag your feet. I could no longer do that, I had to change. Sometimes we are the hindrance to our own prayers coming to fruition; we are not willing to change inwardly in order to see the change outwardly.

Prayer of deliverance: When you pray this type of prayer you are taking the enemy's (Satan) authority away in your life and walking in your authority as a child of God (born again believer of Jesus). When you come to God with this prayer ask for forgiveness and repent, this puts you back into a good relationship with Him. Satan can no longer legally attack you because you are not walking and living in sin. To start you first acknowledge what Christ has done for you on the cross. Know that these habits have been nailed to the cross with Christ and now you are a new creature by the power of Christ's death and resurrection. Also when you are speaking your heart needs to be contrite and totally surrendered to the will of God. You should now be committed to living a glorifying life unto God. After you have acknowledged what Christ has done on the cross, acknowledge that those sins/habits that you have done are nailed to the cross also, and since Christ is raised from the dead you are resurrected as a new creature also and those things no longer have dominion over you, you have dominion over them. You are no longer controlled by your senses and you are no longer a slave to sin. Speak that you have power and dominion over that habit you have and that it is under your feet in Jesus' name. Make sure to ask the Holy Spirit to fill those spots that those habits/sins left with what is pleasing to Him and praise Him for freedom in Him. After this prayer the enemy will try to attack your deliverance and make you doubt it, but be confident and speak the Word of God; stay prayerful and read your Bible daily (Read 2 Corinthians 10:4-5, 1 Corinthians 2:16, 2 Corinthians 5:17, Romans 6:3-14). Now that I have gone through so many twists and turns in my short life, I can see the hand of God more clearly. I am not perfect and there is so much more that needs to be learned. I encourage you to dig in deeper to find your message. Ask God to lead and comfort you using these great scriptures and more. I obeyed the voice of God and now I have a blog (www.hartwords.com), Facebook page (God's Hart), Instagram (@hartwords), and will have a book coming out July 2018. Also find me on social media using #Godshart and #Hartwords. I can truly say that God reached down and helped me to move forward and embrace His plan and turn my mess into a message. Be blessed.

About the Author
Dannielle Hart

Dannielle Hart is the daughter of a pastor and mother who's a devout prayer warrior. She is also a mother to a beautiful teenage daughter. She is from a small town in central California. She holds a Bachelor' of Science degree in Biology from the University of Alabama at Birmingham. She has always enjoyed writing and research and after she graduated college she was led to write a book. She currently writes a blog, www.hartwords.com, a Facebook page, God's Hart, and Instagram, @hartwords. She can also be found on social media through #Godshart and #hartwords. All of her social media and endeavors are meant to draw people to the knowledge of God and to build up the people of God. She aspires to help others enhance their understanding and application of the Word of God into their everyday lives. She has an upcoming project being released in July 2018.

"Balance"

By
Anonymous
Male, Age 48
Las Vegas, NV

(Chapter taken from "Deep Within I Knew He Wasn't for Me- released October 2015)

"Balance"

I have had only a couple serious relationships. Just because we've been seeing each other for three weeks doesn't mean we're in a relationship. Most of my dating history revolved around hooking up and being able to do it again with no pressure. In my relationships, I was faithful. The one woman I thought was worthy of losing myself to, I let get away because I wasn't ready.

What I have learned from my personal experience and coaching others is balance. Now this word is often used but rarely practiced. It has different meanings, but I will focus on the one that should be sought after when pursuing and maintaining a relationship: to bring into harmony or proportion.

This harmony and proportion or disproportion, starts at the very beginning. For example, I was in the comedy club one night with a few drinks in me. A nice looking woman walks by and her frame caught my attention so I talked to her and said "hey." She turned around, a quick conversation ensued and we met up later that week. We had a lot of conversation but no sex. Now at this point, I wasn't looking for a relationship neither was she.

We would see each other often and I had this wonderful plan where we did not need to be exclusive but used protection when away from each other (oh you thought I was going to try and make another person look bad. No! Sometimes it's you, stupid). In the beginning, this piss poor plan was working, but of course it was the beginning! Anyway, I went out of town on business and during a phone conversation the L word came up! If only it had been the L word for lesbian. This instantly changed the dynamics of the relationship for several reasons (but I will keep it short): 1) I didn't say it back, and 2) I questioned her sincerity in using those words.

Now it had only been a couple of months and for me, love isn't something you can give and take back. I don't say it unless I mean it out of respect for those I do that feel that way about and the dignity it carries. All the love is unconditional and it does come with obligations; otherwise it's meaningless. Anyways, we weren't there yet and that's the short truth of why I didn't say it back. Foolish me, not only did I leave this woman out on a limb all by herself with love, I had the audacity to tell her to write down her feelings, the pros and cons of why she loved me. The reason for this was because I knew she didn't really love me. Yeah that's me, not only do I know how I feel but I also know how you feel and why. Yes, arrogance is one of my traits, too.

Now the relationship was off balance. At this point both parties wanted to assign blame either to justify their feelings or take the blame and try to return things to "normal." At that time in my life, I was and can still say I am a work in progress. An arrogant hardliner! She had messed up my good work by saying she loves me! Doesn't she know the importance I put on that word? (Oh no.) Why was she doing this to me? (She was not "doing" anything to you, she's telling you how *she* feels!)

When I got back to town things were weird. I can't tell you how she felt but hurt and anger were probably two, and I was numb and confused. The conversations we had were strange because we did really like each other, but we were clearly on different pages. So we stopped seeing each other for a little while. This added up to about two months. When we started seeing each other again, we picked up where we left off but even stronger. I expressed some deeper feelings and so did she. It was just like the beginning, and that was one of the many problems. You see, we never fully addressed our differences well enough to move forward.

Having differences isn't the problem, its 1) where those differences are 2) whether they are the kind both parties can live with or get over, and 3) if anyone is willing to change. The last one is the only one you have control over as to yourself, and is something you do to better yourself and the relationship, not to make someone else happy.

These differences don't always bear themselves out in the beginning. It's the beginning! This is why it's so important to take your time even if they don't want to. You need time to see who you're dealing with; meanwhile they get the same opportunity. This is dating while you're in or looking for a relationship, not just hooking up.

Looking back, I was saying "Yes, let's see each other more because I do like having you around," but for her it was probably more like "This is it! I want you now and forever!" I'm only basing this on the events that followed later, because in less than three months she was pregnant (dun, dun, dun)! Yes, s*** just got real.

Now this brought a whole new set of problems into an already tenuous situation. I say tenuous because to me all relationships are by definition tenuous until hardships prove otherwise. Who she is or was as a person at that time has nothing to do with the fact that in my mind and by any reasonable account, we were not supposed to be bringing a child into the world at *that* time together.

At the time we had known each other for less than a year. In fact, it had been only about nine months, four of which we had spent apart. There was no talk of marriage, we did not live together, and she already had seven year old son that needed more than a little consideration. There had been a discussion about any possible pregnancy prior to this. Before becoming pregnant she said she would have an abortion. Once she got pregnant, she changed her mind. She gave me a number of

"Balance"

reasons why, but long story short she just "couldn't" have an abortion. I would later come to understand and more than appreciate this later (I love her for it). Meanwhile, I was angry, pissed, stressed, confused, and more than a little panicked. She lied! She was changing our (most importantly, my) lives. We ain't ready for this, why is she doing this to us, most importantly me?

I threw many stones at that woman at the start; it's embarrassing to think of who I was then. Yes she did lie and change her mind, but I gave her the chance to do that. Who didn't wear a condom? Me, that's who! As mad as I was at her, I was ten times as mad at myself for not taking control over the one thing that I knew I had complete control over: me!

For the first four months, I pouted and pissed on her apparent happiness and unexplained joy she seemed to be getting from this whole pregnancy experience. I still wanted an abortion (yeah a real a**hole). You see, what wasn't apparent on the surface was that I had/have trust issues and her change of heart, lie, or whatever you want to call it only exasperated these deep-seated feelings to no end.

Eventually, our issues still unresolved, we moved forward. About six months into her pregnancy, I moved in. Everything was good and we both wanted a healthy mom and baby.

"Balance"

Things weren't perfect but they were far from the place they had been, and four months later we had the most beautiful baby boy known to mankind.

I always wanted a wife before children. Even though I wasn't a husband, I still wanted to be a good dad, a father. At this point she was the mother of my child, not my "baby mama." Our son allowed us to work on one accord for a while. It was a short while. Sooner rather than later, the mother of my child needed me to not just love her but to be "in love" with her. Personally (since you're talking about me), I've always been circumspect, a little hesitant if not all-out distrustful when it comes to being "in love," especially when it comes to a man being "in love" with a woman.

There's no science to back me, but I have come to believe that it is best for a woman to seek a man who loves and respects her. To have a man or woman who is in love with you can lead to some dangerous situations and outcomes. Some would probably explain those situations of obsession or possessiveness. They may be right, but the person acting that way would talk about how "in love" they were. Besides, what argument can you have to being loved and respected? I can still disrespect you in the bedroom when you need or want it.

Anyway, I just couldn't tell her I was "in love" with her because I didn't feel that way and I didn't think she was "in love" either.

"Balance"

I needed answers, real tangible proof. I just can't trust your feelings and emotions because they change. I had never told a woman I was in love with her either. As I stated already, I didn't really trust that. On the other hand, she had these feelings and emotions before, even planned a child and delivered that promise with someone else she was "in love" with. She had already had that previous six year relationship in which at some point she told them she was "in love" with them too. So my question was, what makes me any different?

Don't crucify me yet, we had some good times too. I wasn't always so difficult to deal with. In fact, for all the problems I saw at the time (some real and some imagined) there was one that concerned her the most. Security! Now she never said this word when we talked about it, but it was truly one of the things she wanted most. Oddly enough, I felt the same in that I asked myself a question (not consciously): "Is this a person that I can (and will) trust with all my heart (and life)?" But before we get to that answer, breaking news, pregnancy number two! No, I'm serious!

In my world, babies and small children are loved, period. All of mine are going to get that from me unequivocally. Not just because I'm supposed to, but because they deserve it. My family is the same way; we are far from perfect, but we are very loving. So 14 months after the birth of my first child, we

"Balance"

welcomed a new baby, the most beautiful baby girl known to mankind.

With two babies in less than two years, a significant amount of pressure was put on me to be in love (well duh). But as for me, I was concerned I was already deeply in love with the only people I trusted with it: my kids. I quickly came to realize that the relationship with my kids would suffer if things continue down the same path. Also, I did love her (my baby momma), so I decided to give things a possible chance at success.

There were some things that needed to be cleaned up in my life on a personal level. So I set a time limit to be done with those things, about six months, and focus more on any and all positive things in my life; most importantly my children and their mother.

In my mind, if the difference between us having a happy life and being in love was me, I would change the selfish parts of me to give that a chance. I was the only one I had control over. Anyway, if she's true, she will be; if she ain't, she won't be. Besides, going back to school to give my business plan a better chance at success was a good decision. Slowing down on alcohol made me an all-around better person. Being fully committed in words and deeds (the words that were lacking) to her and my kids made for a happier life for us all.

"Balance"

But what's that saying, "men plan while God laughs?" Well I don't know if he was laughing at me or disappointed, but some unforeseen circumstances blew everything up. Love proved to be less than its claim, because when it could have been put into action and show up, it was absent.

Now all this started with me telling you all about how to pursue and maintain balance while in or pursuing a relationship (ha!); and just like relationships I've been all over the place. But that's just it; matters of the heart don't often reap rational decisions. That's normal, but you just can't stay in an irrational state with unreasonable expectations from the other person or yourself. But it is important to know what you want and where to look for it. Balance ain't so much what you're reaching for but what you are standing on.

So build a solid foundation under yourself. This has less to do with not caring what anybody thinks and more about caring about what's important. While doing that, know that you are worth getting to know and so is (or should be) anyone you desire to be with. When you truly decide to be in a relationship with someone, there is loyalty and obligations that come along with that. You both have a responsibility to nurture that. No one person can carry the responsibility of the relationship by themselves, though one or both may be called upon to do so for a time. That's love, that's real, that's life! Remember that song "Lean On Me?" Yeah!

Once the two of you have established a solid foundation with each other together and you are true to it, if that person goes off the reservation for any reason or "whatever" reason, that has nothing to do with you. You are not to blame, it ain't your fault. If you forgive, forgive; if you don't, then don't. Don't blame yourself! Your love is a reflection of *you* and theirs a reflection of them. My love can influence, but it is not the arbitrator of another person's actions. My love is patient, kind, caring, forgiving, and fearless among other things (though I'm not always). What is yours? We don't have to be exactly alike for our attributes of love to match up.

You can't just push through what you want and think just because you really *like* someone means you love them. In fact, you probably don't even "like" them; you just like how they make you feel. Love doesn't conform to us, we give ourselves to it. Life is a beautiful mess and relationships can be the dirtiest part, but it's the ways they clean us up that is important and should be celebrated.

As for my story, it's not over, but I am available. My kids are my best gifts and I wouldn't trade them for the world. They are the best part of the world and inspire me to be a better person. Now that's love!

"THE LIVES HE LIVED"

By

Tanicia "Shamay Speaks" Currie

Age 35

Bay Area, California

(Chapter taken from "Deep Within I knew He Wasn't for Me- released October 2015 with additions)

"THE LIVES HE LIVED"

I wanted to title this story "The Liar by Omission," but I decided on "The Lives He Lived." Let me break that down a little bit. The "The Liar by Omission" man is the man who usually lives so many lives and tells so many lies that he actually believes them because he lives them on a daily basis. He is very charismatic and quite charming and down to earth. Everyone in town that knows him would describe him as a very cool person. If you want a movie that puts this in perspective for you, watch "The Other Woman" featuring Cameron Diaz. Remember these types of men are stars in their own movies and they bring along blind female co-stars, if you get what I mean.

I had been single for almost four years but of course I dated a few men within that time period. I had been in recovery from my second open heart surgery so dating anyone was not on my mind. One random night in late October 2011, my cousin texted me and asked if I wanted some company. I thought about it and said why not. The evening came and he arrived with my cousin's friend. We'll call him Shaun. Shaun and I seemed to hit it off instantly. During that night we drove to the store together and had a long talk, and the discussion included men living double lives. He said it wasn't cool, etc. Note: there was a Beyoncé' CD in the car (that should have been the 1st red flag), but he said it was his sister's because she had used his car. Now a while ago, because I didn't want to carry baggage, I decided I was going to trust someone until they proved me wrong. From our conversation I really liked him. Now his story went like this: he was recently single. He had been in a 13 year off/on relationship and he had two sons. He stated his ex was partially moved out and their lease was ending. We exchanged numbers that evening and a few days later, he texted me. We chatted through text and planned a date. After that day, I asked a few people that knew him what he was about. I received all good reviews and they all stated he was single. We went on our first date and he was such a gentlemen. He opened car doors and all, and I thought he's such a gentlemen. We hit it off. We continued to chat and planned the second date and we were intimate on this second date. The intimacy was amazing and it seemed like he hadn't had sex in a while; moreover, that's why I felt he wasn't seeing anyone.

Now Shaun was a mechanic so I knew that when I texted he couldn't always reply right away, so I never made a fuss about his late replies. Plus, he literally worked at the shop a block from my grandmother's house. During the time we dated I lived in Sacramento which was an hour away so, I would see him 2-4 times a week when I was in town visiting for business, etc. I hosted events at a nightclub, so on the weekends I would be out very late. There would be times I wouldn't be able to see him because I was running my business but he would usually stay up late to see me. It would be late when we spent time together due to my schedule so when he would doze off, I totally understood that he was tired. I even gave him the nickname "Dozer" because he dozed off in front of me, from being tired from "work." There were a few times when I would text him goodnight, etc., and he would not reply. The next morning, he would usually say he fell asleep (2nd red flag). Remember, during the time we dated, I lived an hour away so I would only be in town 2-4 days at a time. When I was in town, we spent every free minute we could together. I would go see him at work and he would visit me all the time. Being that I always saw him when I wanted and at his job, I never really thought about him seeing other women. We went on dates and all. Things were going good and after two months, he dropped the "L" word. He said I love you while we were texting one day (3rd red flag). When I saw the message I replied, saying we would have to talk about that in person. A couple days later, we were hanging out and as we said our goodbyes, he said, "I love you and I can tell you in person." After he said it, he gave me the most sensual kiss, it curled my toes. I never said it back because I was still a little thrown off, but as time went on I started to feel the same. I hadn't had a serious relationship in a while so it felt so good to be in "love." At that point, we didn't have official labels but we knew where we stood, or at least I thought we did (4th red flag). He would say things that insinuated that we were in a relationship so I didn't worry much about it. Shaun's claim from day one was that he had just left that 13 year relationship, so I didn't care to rush him (5th red flag). I gave time because I know how it is from my past experience; I remember how much time I needed after my last relationship. I believe, even more so now, that people should take time to work on themselves before getting into new relationships. Plus, I wasn't sure that I wanted a full relationship and felt I may need more time but I loved him. I met his mother a couple times and hung out with her, and she even mentioned us having kids. Things were still going good and for Christmas, he gave me a gold necklace with a heart and a key charm. He said it was because he has the key to my heart, and I thought it was the sweetest thing. Our friends and family used to make comments like you guys are so in love because he was so affectionate with me all the time, etc. Shaun and I even talked about having kids in the future. I didn't have any kids yet because I wanted marriage first. Shaun already had two kids, one estranged. After dating for three months, one morning he woke up late and said he had to leave to go visit his friend in jail. I thought that's odd, he never mentioned having a friend in jail. I didn't question it but definitely made a mental note of it. Right after that, I caught the flu and Shaun took off work to bring me soup and medicine. When I think back, those first three months were probably the honeymoon stage.

Right before Valentine's Day, I started getting these harassing private number phone calls, up to 36 calls in one day. It got the point that I had to a file police report. Why would the person never say anything? I thought it could be anyone since my number was on thousands of event flyers yet it was extremely odd. My number had been public for years, especially for business. Long story short, these harassing calls went on every day for over three months. Note: Shaun's phone would always ring but he would say it was customers. I became really frustrated and had to confront Shaun because I knew only an upset woman would play these phone games. Only someone with too much time on her hands would be doing this. He claimed he was not dating anyone else and had no clue. Hmm, we'll get back to that later (6th red flag). Our relationship started to kind of change and I was out of town a little more, dealing with family stuff as I was raising my teenage brother. It seemed like every time I felt we needed to spend more time together, Shaun would always make time and make it up to me. I now realize he was very good at short term satisfaction (7th red flag). Even though I started to feel different, I loved him and the sex was the bomb.

During mid-May, when I was starting to push away, we spent three great days together. Note: at this point since the shop closed, Shaun was a "Busy Mobile Mechanic." I was starting to move and Shaun promised to help but he "got stuck at work" (8th red flag). After this, I decided I was done with him. I decided this mainly because I felt something was off and those harassing calls were still happening. I didn't see Shaun for a full month but he kept contacting me and asking me to talk to him. I refused because I wanted to leave him alone and I didn't see the point. On June 12, I officially moved to my hometown which is where he lived. Right before I moved an older woman added me on Facebook, and I went through her profile pictures. I must have sent her a request so many months prior that I forgot because I didn't even remember sending it. I later found out that she had recently been released from jail. Interestingly enough, when I discovered the release date, my calls abruptly stopped two weeks before that date; furthermore, until this day I still wonder who that was. I am sure we can piece that together because there are really no coincidences in life. The Facebook friend request was accepted about a week after my harassing calls finally stopped. As I looked through her profile pictures, I noticed a picture of her and Shaun from about a year prior (9th red flag). This was extremely odd because remember he was supposed to have been in his previous 13 year relationship at the time of that picture.

Although I was done with Shaun, the day I moved out there, he contacted me. He asked to see me and I was pretty done, but great sex didn't sound too bad. Don't judge me. We hung out and he spent the night, and he kept saying how much he missed and loved me. Little did I know everything was about to come together full circle and make sense, but not total sense. After we woke up that next morning, I asked him who the woman was who added me on Facebook. He said it was a friend (10th red flag). I said, "Hmm, okay," but since I decided that I wasn't dating him anymore, I let it go. It was over, or so I thought. A week later, I was on Facebook and the first thing I saw in my news feed was a picture of him and the older woman with the quote, "Love is in the air." Keep in mind, Shaun was still relentlessly pursuing me. I looked at the comments on the picture, and even his mother commented. I thought that was odd because his mom knew of me, though she didn't know I stopped dealing with him. I immediately called Shaun to ask about this, because I thought we were grown enough to be honest and we didn't have protected sex. I gave him three hours to call me back before I contacted this woman. One thing is, social media tells all and it's like a mini background check. I started to think, well if this woman was around during his last relationship, she must have been a total side chick (11th red flag). This was also a sign that he must have been living a double life because he was in a 13 year relationship back then, right? But where did this woman come from? Well a week later, I found out I was pregnant. Imagine the shock I was in, even though I was done with him, learning he lied since day one and then finding out I was six weeks pregnant. It was too much, especially since I didn't want kids until marriage and with what I just discovered. I could write a full book about my pregnancy, but we'll save that for later.

A month and a half later, after a nightmare month full of drama and extreme life changes, I discovered I wasn't the only one pregnant (12th red flag). This confirmed what I said earlier about the lives he lived. Note: the other pregnant woman was not the ex or the older woman from Facebook. So let's tally that up, he was living four lives that I'd discovered so far. Of course, he said he didn't know if it was his baby, the condom broke, and he was drunk, blah blah. I was totally shocked by hearing of another baby but I was not shocked for long. About a month after, I happened to be on Facebook and saw a picture of his car in my news feed; I guess a mutual Facebook friend of mine had commented on this picture. I clicked on the picture and what do you know, it was a woman's Facebook. I read the comments and that revealed yet another relationship, so that now adds up to five lives he was living. I guess the car he was driving was hers and she had also recently found out about the older woman in jail. Super long story short, he denied everything and said he still loved me. It was pretty laughable, but being pregnant and dealing with all this was no laughing matter. I had this precious little girl who was going to need me and I realized that he wasn't going to be more than what he was now. If he couldn't keep up with all these lives he lived, how could he be a father to these two babies coming? I knew that I did not want to be with him, period. I was extremely disappointed in myself for dating him, for getting pregnant, but mostly for getting pregnant and not being able to have the family I always dreamed of.

There were so many emotions I had to deal with; it made my pregnancy pretty stressful. I was beginning to get more stressed and disappointed each time I found out more bad news, but I had to contain my stress because I have a heart condition. I had just recovered from my 2nd open heart surgery not even a year prior. One day after I discovered he had another child on the way, I had to leave work because I was so upset and in tears. I came home and sat on my porch, four months pregnant, contemplating an abortion. How could I not stick with my plan of waiting for marriage? I made it all the way to age 30, only being pregnant once before at age 17. You see, I got pregnant at 17 in my first toxic relationship but I ended up having a miscarriage. After the miscarriage I made a vow to myself that I would not have children without being married and here I was, pregnant in this situation. I longed to do it "the right way". Why me, right? I knew I could never have an abortion but my mind was lost, sitting on my porch that evening. These are those moments that make you understand why God saved sex for marriage. As I wiped away that last tear, I do feel that God spoke to me, telling me to pick my head up and stop crying. Through all this, I discovered I needed to be accountable for my choices in this. I think as women we sometimes tend to blame the men instead of taking some level of accountability, because it takes it two to tango, as they say. I chose to be with him and I didn't take enough time to really get to know him. He put on an Oscar-worthy act for months, but like they say if it's too good to be true, it probably is. I got pregnant due to taking antibiotics which made my birth control ineffective; however, I could have used condoms.

The harshest reality in all this was realizing my part in it, realizing that I wasn't being careful with my heart or life. Yes, I was single for four years prior to him, but I wasn't really following my heart when dating. Reflecting is something we all must do as people to realize what we could have done differently. Just because you enjoy someone's time doesn't mean they are the one. Just because sex is good doesn't mean you shouldn't protect your body and your heart. The rude awakening I had was that I had values yet I wasn't living by any of them. When you don't live your life aligned with your values, you're destined for failure, especially in the love department. I told myself I did not want to date anyone who wasn't established, yet I continued to date him after he moved in with his mom. If you remember earlier in the story, I mentioned I left him alone for a month. I knew something was off but I should have followed my heart earlier on. I love my daughter and I would go through everything again just for her; however, I wouldn't wish this situation on my worst enemy. All those red flags I missed added to my negative relationship experiences, and made me realize I wasn't living up to my own values. He was my eye opener from God, because God knew something had to wake me up for me to change. I truly feel that God showed me that he was going to give me the best blessing ever, but not without giving me a life lesson. I had to do some extreme soul searching, which I am still doing. It took all this plus my bad experiences over the course of 14 years to realize I didn't love myself enough. I allowed many things to occur that went against what I valued in a relationship, which went against what I knew I was worth. I had been ignoring the messages God had been sending me. If I wanted a husband, why was I dating so carelessly? If I wanted marriage before children, why was I not being more careful? If I wanted real love, why didn't I give myself more time to get to know him before giving him my love? I learned that life will keep sending you messages to show you that you are not living right or show you that you do not love yourself enough. My bad dating choices were showing me that I was continuing to not make the right choices. It took me becoming a single mom, which was one of my biggest fears, to realize that my actions didn't follow my heart or core values.

God's biggest blessing turned out to be my biggest lesson. My baby is such a blessing and I am happy to say her father and I are now great co-parents. He's not perfect by far, but no one is. It's all about how you deal with it and having boundaries. I love that I was able to let things go for the best interest of my child, because it can be challenging being mature while mending a broken heart. I was bitter for a while before I decided to be truly accountable, forgive, and move forward.

We can keep ourselves in emotional bondage if we choose to stay lingering in those feelings of unforgiveness, anger, bitterness, and disappointment, etc. Her father made me learn about myself and what I wanted, so I thank him for that. I thank him for stepping up and being a father. Now his personal life is his issue, but he's turned out to be a better father day by day. I pray for him daily that he will experience more and more personal growth each day. I thank God for pulling the blinders off my eyes, which has helped me to learn to love me first. From all that, I decided I would not be the bitter baby mother, but it did take me time to get to that place and I still struggle with the ups and downs of co-parenting.

No matter how I struggle and no matter what I think he should be doing as a father, now that I am stronger in my faith, I know whatever he doesn't do is between him and God. What I do is my part, meaning that I allow God to deal with him as much as possible. Yes, I get angry at times; I am that mother who is not perfect but I am also that mother who believes in fathers being in their children's life even if they are not perfect. I am that mother who will do my part as a mother and allow my child to decide how she feels about her father. She loves her daddy and I am happy that she does. You will not see me speaking badly about him in front of her, period, as I don't believe in soiling children's minds with adult feelings. I choose not to play God with co-parenting and so far, it's not perfect but it works for me and my peace of mind, which makes me a better mother. I am here now and my daughter is four years old and my baby loves her dad, and I have a peace in my life with co-parenting. Again, it is not perfect but my peace of mind and me showing my daughter love, despite my adult feelings, is what matters. To all you single mothers out there, believe that God turns messes into messages. Be the mother who does her part, don't be bitter, and allow God to deal with what the other parent isn't doing. Don't down talk the other parent in front of your child and don't play God. I could go on for days about what I have learned through co-parenting, trust me. But trust that God will handle it for you even if you don't see it. Yes, you have to go through things to learn sometimes, but if you do not love yourself first, you will never be happy with anyone. You control your outcome and your destiny despite the cards you were dealt. I learned it all starts with you!

You can purchase my full *"Deep Within I Knew He Wasn't for Me"* book at www.ShamaySpeaks.com

The Take Away (Epilogue)

To end this amazing book, I thought it would be awesome to point out some words of wisdom, or messages, featured in each story. There is definitely more than one message in each story. This book features amazing people from different walks of life. In my experiences, I believe wisdom is a purely internal thing as we learn lessons at all ages, but the wisdom we gain from learned lessons is the beauty added to the message.

Discovering My Purpose

"Elementary to High School" By Holly Bella

"The one thing that was constant in my life was listening and being supportive. I was too willing to listen, too willing to guide, and I had nothing left for me. I had all these "ideals" and yearning for what I wanted in my life, yet it was easier to guide people to their destiny instead of listening and guiding myself toward my own."

"It's funny how we can talk ourselves out of the very place GOD is leading us to. Some people are more grounded in their vision and move towards it knowing that the rest will fall into place with no FEAR, just FAITH."

Broken to Resilient

"I Rise" by Briggette Rockett"

I was once told I had no backbone, but I think my struggles have differently strengthened me and my backbone. I have risen above obstacles that should have taken me out and proven statistics wrong on the fatality rate of young teenage mothers. There has been a world of hurt that has entered my soul and it took a lot for me to navigate through it, but I am stronger and wiser for it. Never Should Have Made It, by Marvin Sapp, that is absolutely right. "

"Today, I stand as a woman of strength, with integrity and wisdom, knowing God has given me the heart, backbone, grace and faith to push on despite all the attacks on my mind, body, and spirit. Even at this stage of my life, I am continuously learning and growing, not letting anything or anyone hold me back from allowing me to spread my wings and soar."

If My Story Inspires One Person Then My Job is Done

"God Moments" By Vanessa Oden

"There are moments that are seared into us so deeply that they are etched across our memories and become indelible. Moments that we experience God in such a tangible way that we literally feel the presence of God. Moments that our hearts burn inside of us, and we know without a shadow of a doubt that we have encountered the Divine. I call these God Moments, moments that are undoubtedly God ordained."

"When we take the time to open our physical and spiritual eyes we can start to notice times where God's spirit is moving and where God is showing his Glory. These God Moments leave us with a sense that God was in our midst and that God is with us along every step in our journey. Take time to look for the God Moments in your life, and share them as a testimony to those you encounter along your journey. You never know what spark you light in them. In doing so you just might make a lasting positive change, and if you have inspired just one, you have started a positive chain reaction that could potentially inspire and change the world!"

My MESS turned into My MESSage

"Walk of Worship" By Ben Rivera

"Even then I didn't believe God was working in my life. I was doing it on my own. I was still struggling with my faith in God or even believing in God. Here I was, in church, struggling to believe, and on the worship team. This is one patient God to take me as I am and slowly use music to build my relationship with him. So slowly but surely God and I started having a relationship. I can't tell you the day or when it happened, but it did happen. Through worship God became part of my life. As I look back on this story and the different turns, ups, downs, and just defiance, God has been there. He has put people in my life, whispered ideas, used my passions for His glory. This is the God I love. The God of relationship, who desires us to be in relationship with Him. Who with an open heart will use us as we are and change the world for someone we didn't even know"

"The Beginning of a Destiny Begins With Tearing Down"

By Dannielle Hart

"He had to change these things so that I could live according to His plan and have it stick. He was breaking up the old foundation I had formed my misshapen reality on in order to build a new foundation that He could properly build upon. He took from me the old to make room for His new."

"Sometimes it takes years to find your way. Some people learn faster than others according to our standards, but God knows our individual learning curves. He knows what makes us tick and what we will respond to. In order for a person to change there is always a series of events that occurs that culminates into a reversal of attitudes and ideals that effect how they respond to their surroundings."

"Now that I have gone through so many twists and turns in my short life, I can see the hand of God more clearly. I am not perfect and there is so much more that needs to be learned. I encourage you to dig in deeper to find your message."

"Balance"

By Anonymous

"But that's just it; matters of the heart don't often reap rational decisions. That's normal, but you just can't stay in an irrational state with unreasonable expectations from the other person or yourself. But it is important to know what you want and where to look for it. Balance ain't so much what you're reaching for but what you are standing on."

"You can't just push through what you want and think just because you really like someone means you love them. In fact, you probably don't even "like" them; you just like how they make you feel. Love doesn't conform to us, we give ourselves to it. Life is a beautiful mess and relationships can be the dirtiest part, but it's the ways they clean us up that is important and should be celebrated."

"The Lives He Lived"

By Tanicia "Shamay Speaks" Currie

"As I wiped away that last tear, I do feel that God spoke to me, telling me to pick my head up and stop crying. Through all this, I discovered I needed to be accountable for my choices in this. I think as women we sometimes tend to blame the men instead of taking some level of accountability, because it takes it two to tango, as they say. I chose to be with him and I didn't take enough time to really get to know him."

"The rude awakening I had was that I had values yet I wasn't living by any of them. When you don't live your life aligned with your values, you're destined for failure, especially in the love department."

"It took all this plus my bad experiences over the course of 14 years to realize I didn't love myself enough. I allowed many things to occur that went against what I valued in a relationship, which went against what I knew I was worth. I had been ignoring the messages God had been sending me."

"I was bitter for a while before I decided to be truly accountable, forgive, and move forward. We can keep ourselves in emotional bondage if we choose to stay lingering in those feelings of unforgiveness, anger, bitterness, and disappointment, etc."

Support Your Local Small Businesses:

Become a Published Author!!

Let Shamay assist you!

Join Write It Away Publishing's next book compilation, releasing early 2018!

More Information about book compilations and self-publishing workshops, visit:

Www.WriteItAwayPublishing.Com

Contact Shamay with Write It Away Publishing today!

925-421-0221

ShamaySpeaks@gmail.com

Here's what some of the amazing featured authors have to say:

"I would like to thank you from the bottom of my heart, Shamay, for coaching me to become a first time author! Your workshops from start to finish was so informative. You made sure that I had all the resources that I needed to become an author, I would refer any aspiring author's out there to work with you. You were professional, hands on, and very personal. Thank you for also ensuring a safe, fun, loving environment for me to be successful. Blessings to you. Warm Regards," Andrea McCoy-Taylor

"I am so grateful for the experience to work with Tanicia 'Shamay Speaks' Currie on the Breaking Through Barriers book project. She's such an amazing leader, coach and friend. More importantly, Tanicia always go over and above to make sure her client's needs are met 1000%! Thank you again Tanicia, you've made my first book project experience one of lifetime." Kanishia Wallace

"It was great working with Tanicia. She helped me every step of the way during the process of becoming an author; from compartmentalizing my ideas and getting them on paper to marketing my book and getting my first customer." Rachel Edwards

"Shamay has been a joy to work with. From the first time i met her she was very encouraging and pleasant and very clear on the vision and what she expected of me. She was very professional and is a woman of her word. If she says she is going to do something she does it. She was excellent when it came to meeting deadlines and often met them earlier than promised.

Shamay provided a welcoming atmosphere in all of our workshops and provided great resources and snacks (smile). She made herself available in a way that showed her passion for not only her vision but our vision and goals. I definitely trust her to publish my next project and will be reaching out to her."

Thank you Shamay! Love, Monique

Since July 2016, Shamay has been the creative visionary and publisher for these amazing and powerful book compilations:

Released July 9th, 2016

July 9th, 2016 I had an extremely blessed weekend. It really had my spirit full. I appreciate all the awesome words the ladies said about me, made me tear up. Everything meant so much to me. My deepest gratitude to every amazing woman who allowed me to assist them in becoming authors.

#BreakingBarriers #Testimonies #Authors #MakeItHappen #SkyisTheLimit #ShamaySpeaks Www.shamayspeaks.com

Released January 7th, 2017

January 7th, 2017 I had such a blessed day; words cannot express how I feel. Helping others succeed and be able to bless others. I may provide opportunities but these beautiful women give me the opportunity to assist and guide while walking in purpose. Thank you ladies, for choosing me to work with. It's an honor, congratulations! This is just the beginning♥♥ I'm very proud of each of you continue to step out on faith. Love you y'all! Special thanks to everyone who attended...It humbles me so much the whole experience. It's much more than business, it's about changing lives, providing healing, and stepping out on faith to accomplish goals and dreams. Now I really understand what it means when God said esteem others higher than yourself. Shout out and thanks to my amazing friend and business partner Shauny B Smith for the awesome book cover and my phenomenal cousin for the editing Ilesha Coco Graham and Supreme Photography Marcus Wright. Beautiful and perfect song by Taliah Johnson and Ben Rivera. #Blessed #Thankful #Grateful #AssistingOtherAmazingPeople I would love to work with more amazing women, if you want to come become an author in 2017 contact me text your email address to 925-421-0221

Released June 17th, 2017

Congrats to these beautiful women. I am so honored to have worked with you all. I look forward to your individual book launches. You all make the world proud and will change lives. Thank you for choosing me to lead and guide you. I am beyond blessed 💕💕💕. May God continue to lay put your path of success 💕💕💕.

"Broken Into Brilliance" Empowerment Conference and Book Launch

Live your dreams, anything is possible!

Do you have a book that is finished and you want it published without doing all the research and work to self-publish?

Let Write It Away Publishing help you!

Www.WriteItAwayPublishing.Com

Contact Shamay today for more information and publishing packages!

925-421-0221

ShamaySpeaks@gmail.com

9Quota (925) Art and Music Awards where we give recognition to various artists who contribute greatly to the art, fashion, design and music community. This compilation of talented individuals represent the rich culture of our community and shine light on the up and comers in the area. With the support of the community nominating and voting for these people they get a chance to be inspired as well as inspire others. We have been featured on BET, MTV, Vh1, the Contra Costa Times, East County Times, Mercury News, Oakland Tribune, 89.5 FM Ozcat Radio, and 106.1 KMEL. We are well respected by city officials and always comply with the wishes of the community as well as the Pittsburg Police Department.

This event is completed organized and funded by the 9Quota staff. We take pride in our unique approach in contributing to art in the community. We are fortunate enough to present this event in the historic California Theatre located in the beautiful new revived Downtown Pittsburg area. Previously we have held this event is the Lesher Center for arts in Walnut Creek California and also other locations in Brentwood and Concord. Each winner is presented with a trophy with their named engraved on it to personalize the achievement. We thank all of our supporters.

Branches of Community Services

Tanicia Currie – CEO
Founder- Betty Conner
E-mail: communitybranches925@gmail.com
www.branchesofcommunityservices.org
Business Line: (925) 709-4406
Tax ID #- Available upon request

Our Mission:

Our mission is to support the community by providing branches of educational support, resources, and opportunities for personal development. In fulfilling our mission, we hope to encourage the community to create a cycle of giving back to spread a message of universal community empowerment.

Special thanks to our dedicated team:

Danae Braggs, Shauny B Smith, Miranda O' Hare, Marcus Wright, and all of our supportive and loyal sponsors!

www.KnocksmithMagazine.com

It is no surprise that much of today's media has migrated to online platforms, but there are few truly innovative visionaries who recognize that print, images, videos and music are rapidly converging. One of these leaders is Knocksmith Magazine which is bringing all of these mediums and their fans together to experience something profoundly new and unique.

Knocksmith Magazine offers a physical print magazine that is integrated with online music and video services, via QR apps, codes and giveaways. The production team behind Knocksmith Magazine has showcased some of the emerging superstars of the independent hip-hop scene. The insightful interviews are presented as videos that are accompanied by written articles and full page images. This rich, interactive media offers a 360 degree view of the artist that can't be found anywhere else in the music industry. In addition to intimate looks at rising musical artists, Knocksmith Magazine is also the platform of choice for fans to explore the music scene. The exhaustive collection of artists and music found on the Knocksmith Magazine catalogue enables fans to hear new songs, link to download sites and find similar artists. Finally, Knocksmith Magazine is a proud supporter of music lovers. Through their "Save the Record Stores" campaign, the magazine is helping to preserve an important but endangered part of the music industry. That is why Knocksmith Magazine encourages purchase of music both online and through neighborhood record stores.

Need an award-winning great designer for book covers and/or graphic design work:

Contact Shauny B Smith with KnockSmith Magazine: www.KnocksmithMazagine.com

Ben Rivera, One of the amazing featured authors is a part of an amazing band:

5 O'clock Somewhere (Band)

Facebook @5oclocksomewhererocks

http://5oclocksomewhere.rocks/

(707) 249-2567

5 O'clock Somewhere is a local band in northern California playing all your favorite country and rock-n-roll hits. From The Zac Brown Band to ZZ Topp.

Special thanks to my daughter for being EVERYTHING to me, she changed my life forever. Laniyah you are mommy's BEST blessing. Single mommy life is hard but you give me purpose. I will do everything to show you the way and be the BEST mommy I can be! I love you my HoneyBunn! To all the single mommies out there, I know it's hard to pursue your dreams when you are doing it alone; however, never allow everything to hold you back. Single parents go through many struggles but rests assure that God will see you through. Encourage yourself and don't lose sight of your dream despite your struggles!

Children are a blessing and every person has a purpose from birth,

Laniyah you give mommy purpose!

www.ingramcontent.com/pod-product-compliance
Lightning Source LLC
Chambersburg PA
CBHW071118090426
42736CB00012B/1948